D0981625

EXPLORATIONS IN WORLD ETHNOLOGY

ROBERT B. EDGERTON and L. L. LANGNESS
University of California, Los Angeles

General Editors

WEEKEND WARRIORS

Alcohol in a Micronesian Culture

MAC MARSHALL

The University of Iowa

The meaning of alcohol in culture has tended to be a
neglected topic, though the close kinship of meaning and
motivation suggests that it is an important subject
for anyone concerned with alcohol abuse.

J. L. Honigmann, "Alcohol in its cultural context"

 MAYFIELD PUBLISHING COMPANY

To the warriors of Truk, past, present and future.

Copyright © 1979 by Mac Marshall
First edition 1979

All rights reserved. No portion of this book may be
reproduced in any form or by any means without
written permission of the publisher.

Library of Congress Catalog Number: 78-64597
International Standard Book Number: 0-87484-455-X

Manufactured in the United States of America
Mayfield Publishing Company
285 Hamilton Avenue, Palo Alto, California 94301

This book was set in Aster by Chapman's
Phototypesetting and was printed and bound by Malloy
Lithographing. Sponsoring editor was Alden C. Paine,
Carole Norton supervised editing, and Maggie Cutler
was manuscript editor. Michelle Hogan supervised
production, and the text and cover were designed by
Nancy Sears. Photographs not otherwise cited are by
the author. Cover drawing from *The History of Mankind*,
Vol. 1, by Friedrich Ratzel (Macmillan, 1896).

Contents

Preface

During the nineteenth century, the inhabitants of Truk in the eastern Caroline Islands of Micronesia acquired a reputation for ferocity and bravery vis-à-vis foreigners. This bellicose reputation led foreigners to coin an alternative name for Truk that has now fallen largely into disuse: *Dread Hogoleu*. Whether the Trukese were any more violent than other Micronesians or the outsiders who came among them is arguable, but Truk's reputation for inhospitality to strangers caused many foreigners to shun the islands for fear of being attacked. By the early twentieth century, however, under the influence of the German colonial government, the Trukese surrendered all firearms and ceased all warfare. The xenophobia that characterized Truk's relations with the outside world during most of the nineteenth century was only a memory of a bygone age. Or was it?

Truk has once again acquired a fearsome reputation among many foreigners. Now, however, the ferocity and bravery of the Trukese are focused in the consumption of alcoholic beverages and in the drunken brawls that frequently accompany drinking. The nineteenth-century stereotype of the fearless Trukese warrior has been replaced by the twentieth-century stereotype of the fearsome Trukese drunk. Quite clearly, the myth of Dread Hogoleu lives on.

My purpose in this book is to examine contemporary Trukese drinking behavior. I develop the idea that contemporary drunkenness (and its associated fighting) is a modern-day substitute for traditional warfare. This suggestion has been made by several authors (Caughey 1970:118;

Hezel n.d.; Mahoney 1974; Nason 1975:624), but no one has pursued the idea much beyond pointing out the analogy. The importance of the analogy lies not in describing the functions of drinking but rather in drawing our attention to the continuity of certain basic problems and premises in Trukese culture over a century of intensive outside contact.

That drunken brawling may provide a substitute for traditional warfare seems plausible, but merely stating this purported relationship does not explain why and how this state of affairs came to be. What characteristics of Trukese social organization might have contributed to the contemporary style of drinking that many foreigners find so repugnant? Have particular historical influences played a significant role in this process, and if so, can we identify them? Are there any underlying themes in the Trukese world view that inform this matter? It is questions such as these that we explore in this book.

Many scholars who have studied the effects of different drug substances on human beings—including ethanol, the active ingredient in alcoholic beverages—have concerned themselves with altered states of consciousness. My concern here is somewhat different. I am concerned with what we might call altered states of *conscience*. By this I refer to the way that persons who carry a shared culture agree to set aside normal rules for acceptable behavior when a particular drug substance has been consumed. Altered states of conscience allow persons to engage in normally forbidden behaviors without censure, but this does not mean that such behaviors are without pattern or limits. The state of alcohol inebriation is at all times and in all places surrounded by limits, even though these limits are usually more lax than those regularly permitted. My concern in writing about Trukese drunken comportment is not with the physiological effects of ethanol, but rather with what Trukese persons believe about these effects. I am especially interested in how these beliefs influence behavior and what these beliefs and behaviors reveal about the Trukese world view.

I distinguish between *alcohol abuse* as socially disruptive behaviors associated with the consumption of beverage alcohol, and *alcoholism* as physiological or psychological dependency on ethanol which may or may not be accompanied by socially disruptive behaviors. According to this distinction, very few Trukese drinkers are alcoholics, although Truk has a great deal of alcohol abuse (see chapter 4 and Postscript). So this is not a book about alcoholism and addictive drinking. Nor is it a book that focuses primarily on alcohol abuse, although this subject will be touched upon. At one level this is an ethnography of drunken comportment—the style of behavior that Trukese adopt when consuming alcoholic beverages. But at another, more important, level, this is a book about what Bateson (1958) calls *ethos*—the characteristic spirit or sentiment of a people or community, the emotional emphases of the culture. I believe that by delving into Trukese conceptions of drunkenness and its causes and consequences we will reach a better understanding of such core emotional issues as the relationships between the sexes, the expression of aggression, and intergenerational antagonisms. In combination with material already available on Trukese character and on basic Trukese values, this will provide us not only with an explanation for why Trukese drinking is so often disruptive, but also with a clearer idea of how the world appears through Trukese eyes.

This book is an exercise in what Clifford Geertz has called "thick description." It represents an interpretation of my understanding of my informants' interpretations of their own culture. It builds on the quite extensive and impressive array of anthropological material that has been published on the different communities of Truk in an effort to plunge more deeply into some of the problems raised by earlier investigators. Finally, it is an effort at cultural analysis in the sense that it involves "guessing at meanings, assessing the guesses, and drawing explanatory conclusions from the better guesses" (Geertz 1973:20).

The near universal consensus among foreigners familiar with Micronesia and among many Micronesians themselves is that alcohol abuse is a major problem in paradise. Alcohol consumption has become, from this point of view, both the cause and the symptom of many other social problems in the islands. Thus, delinquent behavior is linked to the misuse of alcohol; the search for alcohol or for money to purchase it is considered a prime motivation for theft; alcohol is implicated in many cases of assault, homicide, and suicide; and many young people are said to drink out of sheer boredom or out of frustration over their unemployment or predicament in life.

By the late 1960s, recommendations were being made that the growing problem of alcohol abuse in the district centers had to be "solved." Thus, the U.S. government made funds available to the Trust Territory government. To tap these funds, the Trust Territory government was required to work up an Alcoholism Plan, a task that fell to the Division of Mental Health, Department of Health Services. This plan was first submitted to the National Institute of Alcohol Abuse and Alcoholism in 1974. Subsequent revisions and additions have been made through 1976. In preparing the plan a contract was let to a consulting firm in Washington, D.C., to investigate social and cultural factors involved in alcohol abuse (see Mahoney 1974).

Despite this flurry of recent governmental activity in the Trust Territory, we still know precious little about alcohol use and abuse in Micronesia. Before any sort of meaningful alcohol treatment program can be devised—if, indeed, one is called for—those engaged in this task must have detailed data on drinking behavior and the attitudes and values that surround it for each of the major Micronesian cultures. In writing this book one of my primary goals has been to provide an explanation of Trukese drinking and drunkenness that may assist the Trukese in evaluating the nature of the alcohol problem in their islands. Should they conclude that a problem in fact exists, then I hope this book will contribute in some small way toward finding a solution.

Acknowledgments

The research for this book was conducted over a period of seven months during 1976 in the village of Peniyesene on Moen Island, Truk, in the eastern Caroline Islands of Micronesia. In preparing this volume I have also drawn on earlier field work conducted for eighteen months on Namoluk Atoll, Truk District, between 1969 and 1971, and on an archival study of the history of alcoholic beverages in Micronesia carried out during the summer of 1974. The Peniyesene field work was funded by a Faculty Research Assignment from the University of Iowa and a grant from the American Philosophical Society, Johnson Fund. The Namoluk field work was supported by the National Institute of Mental Health (Predoctoral Research Grant MH11871-01 and Fellowship MH42666-01) and the Department of Anthropology, University of Washington. The archival research was conducted in the libraries of the Bernice Pauahi Bishop Museum and the University of Hawaii and was made possible by Biomedical Sciences Support Grant FR-07035 from the General Research Support Branch, Division of Research Resources, Bureau of Health Professions Education Manpower Training, National Institutes of Health, to the University of Iowa. The specific award that underwrote my work was made through the Graduate Research Council, University of Iowa. Finally, in addition to my genuine appreciation for the above sources of support, I am most grateful to the University of Iowa for an Old Gold Summer Faculty Research Fellowship during the summer of 1977 which gave me the time to write this book.

A number of individuals have materially contributed to this research. Foremost among them is Leslie B. Marshall, co-fieldworker, confidant, editor, and patient critic. I also appreciate stimulating discussions with Father Fran Hezel, S.J., and Dan Foley on alcohol-related topics while in the field. Both of these men provided me with useful documentary sources. The media class at Xavier High School on Truk, under the able direction of Eric Metzgar, generously shared a number of photographs with me, some of which appear in this book. Lew Langness, Robert Edgerton, Carole Norton, and particularly Marjorie Cutler have contributed helpful editorial suggestions which have improved the readability of the text.

The most significant contribution, of course, comes from the people of Peniyesene themselves, to whom my family and I owe a large debt of thanks for their warm hospitality and friendship during the period we lived among them. *Kinisou ami chon Peniyesene ren chonmong umöümöch ngeni kem.*

University of Iowa
August 1977

Editors' Preface

Western societies tend to view drunkenness and alcoholism as essentially one and the same thing. Alcoholism is commonly seen as a personal affliction, a "disease," and its behavioral manifestation, drunkenness, is seen as a societal affliction. In both dimensions, alcohol abuse is regarded as necessarily and inevitably disruptive and undesirable, and wherever it is found programs are instituted to deal with it. Yet to date no medical or psychiatric intervention has met with much success in dealing with problem drinkers who do not "really want to stop." Perhaps it is time we examined more carefully the reasons why so few drinkers are motivated to change. Drinking and drunkenness are rarely, if ever, considered from the broader point of view of how they interrelate with other features of Western society and culture. It is clear, for example, that in many of the same cultures where drinking is regarded as a major social problem it is also widely glamorized and promoted as part of the good life. The cocktail party is as much an American institution as the Fourth of July. Billboards and magazine advertisements tell us that people who are "with it" drink this or that alcoholic beverage. Drinking is portrayed as manly and, increasingly nowadays, womanly as well. What is more, drunkenness is accepted as both an explanation and an excuse for wrongdoing, even very serious wrongdoing. Obviously the factors that influence drinking behavior are extremely complex, and perhaps it is this very complexity that frustrates our attempts to see our own alcohol use in its full cultural context. And here lies much of the value of Marshall's account.

Moen Island, Truk, is a small and pretty much self-contained Micronesian culture in which alcohol abuse is a relatively recent phenomenon and its development is fairly well documented. The Moen experience enables us to see in a way that would be much more difficult in our own case how drinking can become incorporated and embedded into an ongoing cultural system, and how values and attitudes within the system influence the style of drinking and perpetuate it. Marshall's careful analysis also enables us to understand why it is that attempts to solve the "problem" in Micronesia have been in many ways misguided because they are unrelated to the drinking behavior itself as perceived by the participants. Naturally the Moen Island case cannot be generalized to the United States, but it can and does demonstrate that many of our beliefs about drinking and drunkenness may be faulty and that a genuine understanding demands a social and cultural approach as well as a medical one.

Mac Marshall was educated at Grinnell College and the University of Washington, receiving his Ph.D. from the latter in 1972. He is currently an associate professor and acting chairman of the Department of Anthropology at the University of Iowa. Since 1969 he has been conducting research in Micronesia, the results of which have appeared in numerous chapters and articles. In addition to his interest in alcohol and *kava*, he has published on marriage, adoption, incest, fosterage, and, with collaborators, on toxoplasmosis. In addition to this book Dr. Marshall has edited a reader, *Alcohol and Culture*, soon to be published by the University of Michigan Press.

L. L. Langness
Robert B. Edgerton

WEEKEND WARRIORS
Alcohol in a Micronesian Culture

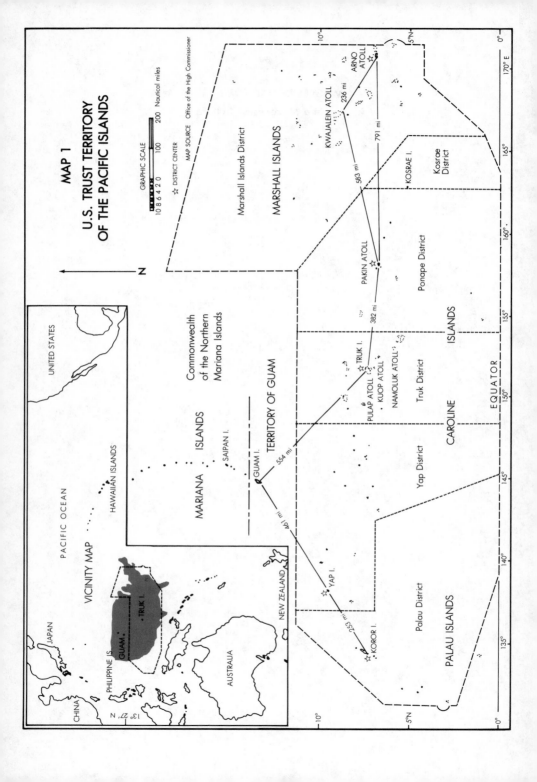

Moen and Peniyesene: The Research Setting

1

> Congressman X was flagged down by a newsman on the steps of the Capitol.
>
> "What are you going to do about Micronesia?" inquired the reporter.
>
> "Mike who?" said Mr. X.
>
> **W. Price,** America's Paradise Lost

ON AIR MIKE TO MICRONESIA

Boarding Air Micronesia's Boeing-727 at Honolulu International Airport, one is scarcely prepared for the typical Micronesian port town, or district center, to be encountered a few hours later. "Air Mike," as the airline is affectionately known in the Trust Territory, links Majuro, Kwajalein, Ponape, Truk, Guam, Saipan, Yap, and Palau to Hawaii with several flights per week (map 1). After a short refueling stop at the U.S. military base on Johnston Atoll, the jet drops smoothly down at Majuro in the Marshall Islands and one is in the "TT." From Majuro, the plane flies quickly on to the U.S. Army's missile test range at Kwajalein, the world's largest atoll.[1] Struck by the lowness and smallness of the islands seen thus far, a first-time visitor to Micronesia is reassured by the mountainous expanse of Ponape, which looks much like the islands of Hawaii. Leaving the "rain garden" of Ponape behind, Air Mike jets westward toward the Lagoon of Truk.

Nothing one has seen yet on the trip rivals the vista Air Mike offers of Truk Lagoon (map 2). An enormous expanse of 823 square miles, nearly

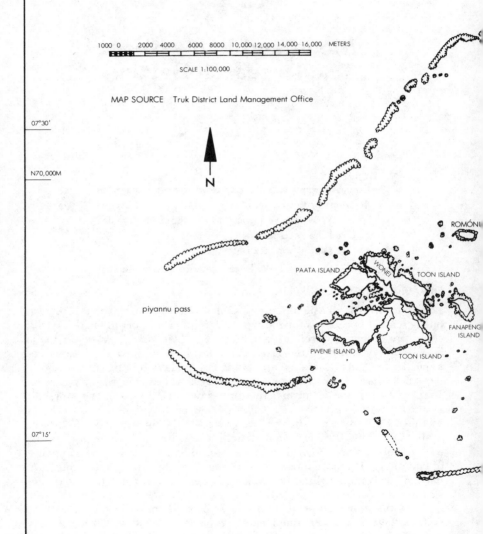

MAP 2
ISLANDS OF TRUK LAGOON

1000 0   2000 4000   6000 8000 10,000 12,000 14,000 16,000   METERS

SCALE 1:100,000

MAP SOURCE   Truk District Land Management Office

N

07°30'

N70,000M

07°15'

ROMÓNU

PAATA ISLAND

WONEI

TOON ISLAND

piyannu pass

FANAPENG
ISLAND

PWENE ISLAND

TOON ISLAND

151°30'

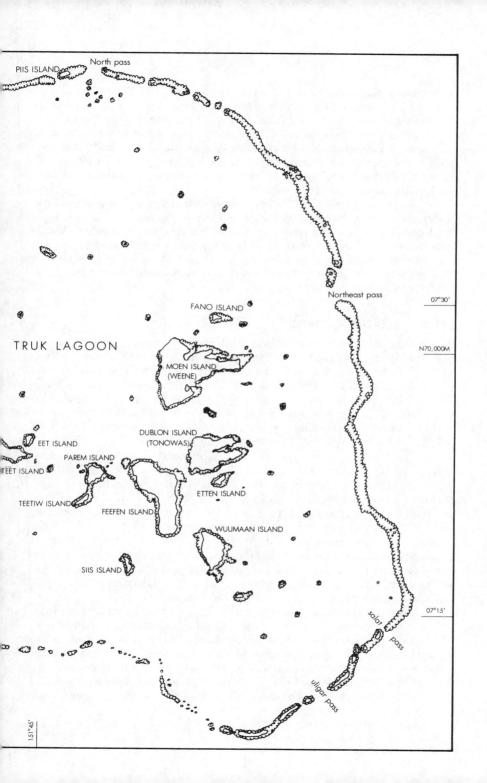

PIIS ISLAND   North pass

TRUK LAGOON

FANO ISLAND

MOEN ISLAND
(WEENE)

EET ISLAND

DUBLON ISLAND
(TONOWAS)

PAREM ISLAND

TEET ISLAND

ETTEN ISLAND

TEETIW ISLAND

FEEFEN ISLAND

WUUMAAN ISLAND

SIIS ISLAND

Northeast pass

salat pass

uligar pass

07°30'

N70,000M

07°15'

151°45'

as large as Kwajalein and ringed with low atoll islets, Truk harbors a fleet of small but verdant high islands. This complex atoll is unique anywhere on earth and is the result of a huge volcanic mountain slowly sinking beneath the sea over eons of time. As the outer rim of this giant mountain has sunk, coral polyps have continuously grown and died and built the wide coral reef that surrounds Truk Lagoon. The dozen or so inhabited high islands that thrust up out of the lagoon itself are the remnants of the peak of this once-great volcano.

Not only is Truk's land form unique, but many will argue that its beauty is too. The interplay of blues and greens on reef, water, sky, and land creates an ever-changing tapestry of breathtaking splendor. Given this physical beauty, one is shocked on disembarking at Moen by the dirt and ramshackle squalor of the port town. But Moen only mirrors the strange juxtaposition of natural beauty and man-made blight that characterizes all of Micronesia's port towns.

MOEN: THE DISTRICT CENTER

The beauty of Moen is found primarily in the Trukese people themselves, but it is also present in the town's tropical verdure, which seems capable of overcoming all but the worst human insults to the environment. In the slang phrase, "Moen grows on you."[2] Most foreigners who remain on Truk for any time become blind to the blight of a rusting car lying next to a stand of pink hibiscus shaded by an immense breadfruit tree, the overwater benjos[3] commanding a panoramic view of sunsets over Truk Lagoon; and the empty beer cans everywhere underfoot.

The rusting automobiles, decrepit toilets, and ubiquitous beer cans symbolize the contact culture life-style of Micronesia's district centers. Many who live in the port towns have enough money to purchase vehicles (primarily Datsuns and Toyotas from Japan), but few have the expertise or facilities to maintain them for more than two or three years before the salt air claims them for its own. Only a small minority of the people living in district centers have access to indoor plumbing, and most resort to Micronesia's traditional lagoon latrines, which flush twice a day. Everyone who wants to drinks Micronesia's new national beverage—beer. As a commentator recently put it: "People who once drank *tuba* now want beer, and they want it cold" (Nevin 1977:31; figure 1).

Moen is an island of just over seven square miles, much of it in near-vertical mountainous terrain, whose highest peak rises 1,214 feet above the lagoon (map 3). The population of Moen has expanded almost exponentially during the American period when compared with the previous twenty-five years. Japanese census reports give Moen's total population as 2,210 in 1920; 2,228 in 1925; 2,295 in 1930; and 2,115 in 1935 (Japan 1931c, 1937). By 1967, this number had more than doubled to 5,687, and

Figure 1. People who once drank palm wine now drink beer

Media Class, Xavier High School, Truk

six years later in 1973 it had nearly doubled again to 9,562 (Kay 1974). In the absence of a formal census, the best estimate is that Moen's present population is in the neighborhood of 11,000 persons. Though small by world standards, the Micronesian port towns bear all the features of urban centers. Relative to the very small number of persons on most outer islands, which often number only a few hundred, Micronesia's "cities" are big indeed.

The district centers are the hubs of activity in Micronesia today, whether that activity be education, employment, entertainment, modern health care, or simply the chance to participate in a new way of life. The attractiveness of this new life-style and the many amenities and opportunities offered by the port towns account in large measure for the rapid growth of the towns over the past fifteen years. While the Trust Territory's population expanded at an annual rate of better than 3.5 percent per year between 1967 and 1973, the population of the port towns increased at a rate of between 5 and 11 percent per year during this same period. This discrepancy is accounted for by immigration to the district centers from the outer islands, especially immigration by young people (see, e.g., Marshall 1975b).

7

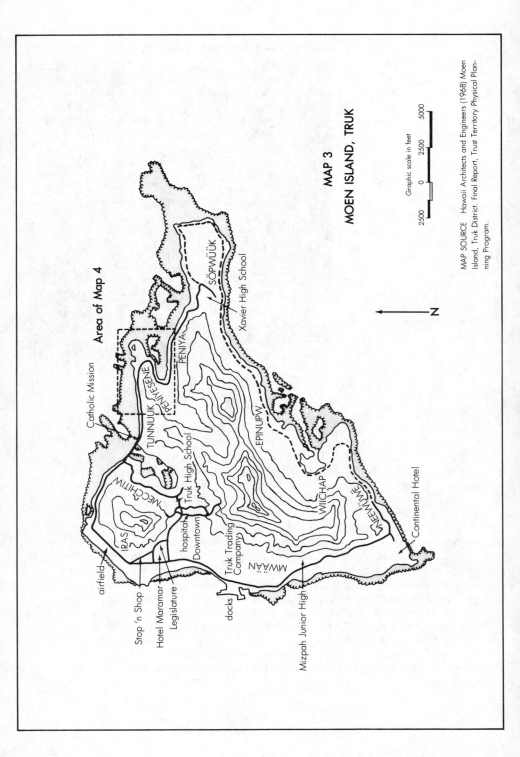

Area of Map 4

Catholic Mission

airfield

Stop 'n Shop

Hotel Maramar

Legislature

docks

hospital

Downtown

Truk High School

Truk Trading Company

Mizpah Junior High

TUNNUUK

PENESENE

MECCHITIW

IRAS

MWÁÁN

PENIYA

SÓPWUÚK

Xavier High School

EPINUPW

WIICHAP

NEÉWÓNNE

Continental Hotel

N

MAP 3

MOEN ISLAND, TRUK

Graphic scale in feet

2500   0   2500   5000

MAP SOURCE Hawaii Architects and Engineers (1968) Moen Island, Truk District. Final Report, Trust Territory Physical Planning Program.

"Downtown" on Moen consists of an area embracing parts of at least three different traditional villages—Iras, Neepwukos, and Mwään—along with the administrative headquarters area on the hill above. Downtown contains most major governmental and commercial facilities and serves as the link between Truk District (map 4) and the rest of the world because it houses the airport, the harbor and docks for shipping, and the radio and telecommunication centers (figure 2). Administrative buildings located downtown include the office of the district administrator, the Truk Dis-

Asia Mapping, Inc., Agana, Guam

Figure 2. Downtown Moen, Truk (January 1976): a, airport runway and terminal; b, Stop 'n Shop store and bar; c, Iras Elementary School; d, Truk District Legislature; e, radio station WSZC; f, office of the district administrator; g, district court; h, Truk High School; i, government housing; j, hospital; k, Bank of America; l, U. S. Post Office; m, Truk Trading Company; n, harbor and dock facility

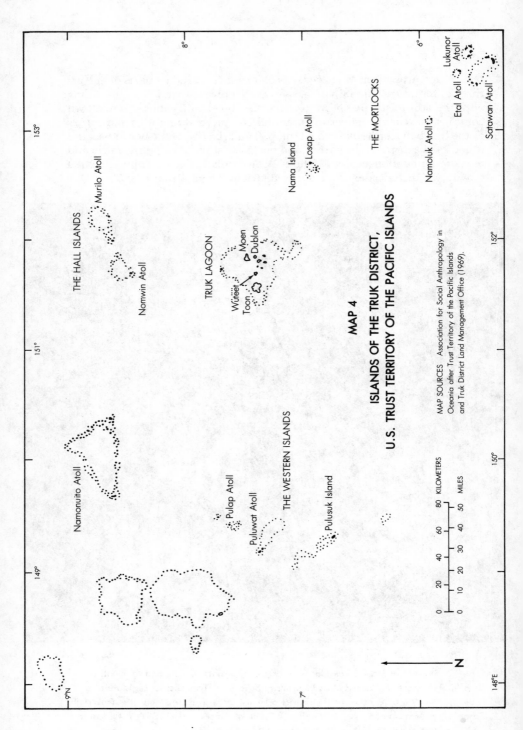

MAP 4

ISLANDS OF THE TRUK DISTRICT,
U.S. TRUST TERRITORY OF THE PACIFIC ISLANDS

MAP SOURCES   Association for Social Anthropology in
Oceania after Trust Territory of the Pacific Islands
and Truk District Land Management Office (1969).

10

trict Legislature, the district hospital, district court chambers, and the offices for other departments such as education and public works. Close by the new multimillion dollar hospital lies the campus of Truk High School, the district's major public educational facility. Also in this area is the governmental housing complex, built originally for Americans hired to work as contract personnel on hardship assignments, and now filled mostly by upper-level Micronesian bureaucrats.

The district's oldest and largest commercial complex—Truk Trading Company (TTC)—has been joined in recent years by a number of modern air-conditioned stores selling everything from hardware to imported food to clothing and locally made handicraft (figures 3 and 4). Prominently displayed on the shelves of most of these stores is a wide array of imported alcoholic beverages. Scattered among these stores and government offices are four small, locally owned hotels, two of which run popular bars; the district's radio station (WSZC); two local produce markets; the Bank of America; and the U. S. Post Office, complete with its own Zip Code. Also located downtown are a large public elementary school, the boat pool,[4] several churches, and a variety of housing ranging from tropical-palatial to ghettolike. The downtown streets are paved, and most persons who live downtown have electricity and running water.

Paved roads cease at the outer limits of the downtown area, and this provides as good a boundary as any for demarcating the town from the suburbs. Electric lines and water pipes run farther than the paved roads, extending as far as the causeway linking Mecchitiw with Tunnuuk on the north and down through Mwään to the Continental-Travelodge Hotel complex at the southwest point of the island. Beyond these points, the roads become much rougher and one passes through areas devoid of housing.

Clambering into the back end of a Truk taxi—a small Japanese pickup truck noisy of muffler and devoid of springs—we hunker down with eight or ten others and brace ourselves for the bumpy half-hour journey required to traverse the five miles from downtown to the village of Peniyesene.

After reaching Mecchitiw, the taxi rides over the narrow causeway that cuts across the bay separating Mecchitiw from Tunnuuk. The buildings of the Catholic mission headquarters and St. Cecelia's Elementary School await those who cross the causeway. Like a medieval European town plunked down in the midst of the blue Pacific, a hodge-podge of homes nestles at the feet of the Tunnuuk cathedral. Rocking at anchor in the nearby roadstead, the Catholic mission vessel, *Star of the Sea*, recalls an earlier era when sailing ships and canoes dominated Micronesian travel.

Figure 3. Stop 'n Shop business complex, Moen, Truk

Figure 4. Moen municipal market and local taxi

From Tunnuuk cathedral, the road seems to grow narrower, and the housing is more spread out as we move through the three internal divisions of Tunnuuk. Suddenly, rounding a sharp curve to the right, a long shallow bay opens before us, ringed with houses. We have reached the village of Peniyesene (figure 5).

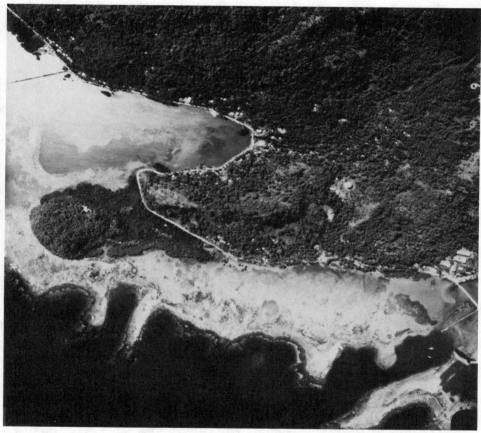

Asia Mapping, Inc., Agana, Guam

Figure 5. Aerial view of Tunnuuk (lower right), Peniyesene (center), and Peniya (upper left) districts, Moen, Truk (January 1976)

PENIYESENE: THE PHYSICAL SETTING

As we round the bend into Peniyesene, a sheer basalt cliff looms fifty feet straight up on the right. The houses in the distance on the other side of the bay belong not to Peniyesene but to its neighboring village of Peniya. Almost without exception, the dwellings in Peniyesene are on the right, nestled up under the cliff and lining the roadway clear to the head of the bay. On the left, jutting out over the lagoon, are the benjos.

Behind the bay and up the river, which is the only continuously flowing stream on Moen, a classic Pacific Island valley rises. Sided by steep, tree-covered slopes that plunge in a sharp V toward the river at the bottom of the valley, much of Peniyesene meanders up the valley's lower reaches (figure 6). Dominating the skyline behind the bay are the two big peaks of Mt. Wiitipwen and Mt. Winifëwürëër.

Along the road to town at the head of the bay lies the center of Peniyesene village life. Here are located the Protestant church, movie theater, poolhall-cafe, and the two largest stores in the community (map 5). These are interspersed among a variety of houses that reflect the emergent class differences based on monetary wealth in the village.

Figure 6. Physical setting of Peniyesene showing Wiichen River Valley and Mt. Winifëwürëër in the background. Houses visible in lower left are located in Peniya

14

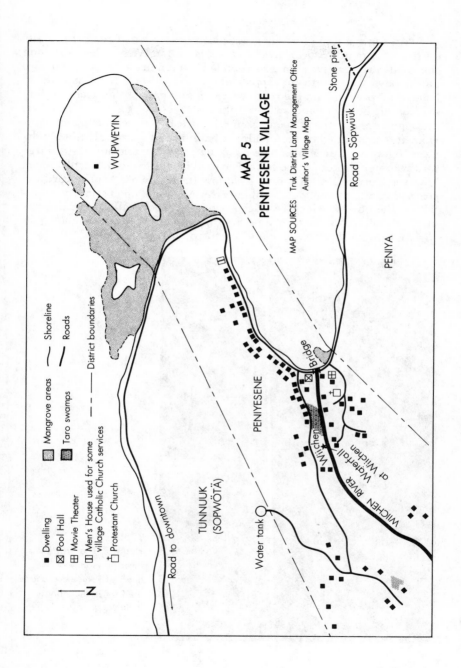

MAP 5
PENIYESENE VILLAGE

MAP SOURCES Truk District Land Management Office
Author's Village Map

Legend:
- ■ Dwelling
- ⊠ Pool Hall
- ⊞ Movie Theater
- ⊞ Men's House used for some village Catholic Church services
- ⌂ Protestant Church

- ▨ Mangrove areas
- ▦ Taro swamps
- — Shoreline
- ▬ Roads
- –·– District boundaries

N →

Labels on map:
WUPWEYIN
PENIYESENE
TUNNUUK (SOPWÖTÄ)
Road to downtown
Water tank
WIICHEN RIVER
Waterfall at Wiichen
PENIYA
Bridge
Road to Sópwüük
Stone pier

An eager group of young guides leads us up a dirt road that splits off from the main road to town and heads up the river valley. All along this road are attractive homes surrounded by breadfruit, banana, soursop, and papaya trees, with pineapples and a myriad of ornamental plants beneath. Proceeding up the road, we catch glimpses of the river gurgling over basalt boulders and swishing through reedlike grasses on our left. Through some of these openings in the brush we see small groups of women accompanied by their children bathing and washing clothes in the river (figure 7). Our guides take us on up the road, and we pass a large taro swamp irrigated by the river. The road begins to climb steeply. Soon, however, our guides beckon us to follow them down a trail toward the river. Abruptly, round a curve in the river, we come upon a lovely waterfall, at the base of which is a deep pool. This spot, called Wiichen, has attracted persons since time immemorial, as evidenced by the many petroglyphs in the sheer basalt cauldron surrounding the pool.

Figure 7. The Wiichen River flows through the heart of Peniyesene and is used for bathing and laundering

On returning to the main road, our guides inform us that it proceeds to other houses that become few and far between further up the valley. We elect to retrace our steps to the vicinity of the poolhall. Reaching the junction between the road to town and the road up the valley, we turn right toward Peniya and poke our heads into the poolhall. Our presence is briefly acknowledged by the half-dozen young men watching two of their number compete at pocket billiards. The poolhall consists of one half of a large room, the other half of which is given over to a small store stocking a variety of canned goods, flashlight batteries, cigarettes, mosquito coils, and the like. Back of the store, separated by a wall, is a small cafe with a few tables and chairs where men gather to drink coffee (figure 8). The cafe does its best business selling *tempura*, rather heavy, somewhat greasy, large doughnuts.

Back on the main road, we hike across the bridge spanning the river's mouth where it empties into the bay. Another store and a huge

Figure 8. The local poolhall-cafe at the mouth of the Wiichen River is the center of social activity for Peniyesene young men

two-story shed that masquerades as a movie theater are on our right, situated where a Japanese-run elementary school once stood (figure 9). All that remains of the school are the steps and the front entranceway, standing a bit forlornly next to the theater where a poster proclaims tonight's attraction to be the kung fu thriller *Game of Death*, starring Bruce Lee.

We wander back of the movie theater past an old Japanese machine gun bunker toward the Protestant church (figure 10). We notice another road meandering up the hill behind the church, but our guides tell us that it stops just a short way beyond. Our brief stroll, coupled with the ride in on the taxi, has allowed us to see most of Peniyesene.

Our impression of the village is one of greenery everywhere, and generally attractive homes, but something seems unusual. Standing by the bridge and reflecting for a moment, we realize that there are not many people around, or, more accurately, only the very young, the very old, housewives, and a few young men have been encountered.

PENIYESENE: A BEDROOM SUBURB

It begins every morning at 6:00 A.M. Taxis loaded with men and women from the outlying villages of Söpwüük and Peniya hurry through Peniyesene, picking up occasional riders along the way. Meanwhile, taxis owned by Peniyesene residents congregate outside the poolhall, race their engines, gather their loads, and head for town (figure 11).

Figure 9. The local movie theater in Peniyesene specializes in kung fu thrillers

Figure 10. The heart of Peniyesene: left, Protestant church (note the old Japanese machine gun bunker); center, the poolhall-cafe; right, dwelling and movie theater

Figure 11. The road to town and Moen's shoreline viewed from the basalt cliff above Peniyesene

19

That Peniyesene is a bedroom suburb of downtown Moen is a point literally driven home every afternoon and evening, when students and wage earners repopulate the village, having commuted out that morning for school or jobs elsewhere on the island. Unlike many other communities in Truk District (map 5), Peniyesene has no village elementary school. Consequently, parents must look elsewhere for their childrens' education. The nearest elementary school, St. Cecelia's, is run by the Catholic mission and is located about a mile and a half away in Tunnuuk. Those who attend St. Cecelia's pay a small fee and need not be Catholic to enroll. The greatest number of Peniyesene's 103 elementary school pupils attend St. Cecelia's (table 1). But Peniyesene's dominant orientation downtown is

TABLE 1
Schools Attended by Pupils from Peniyesene, March 1976

Name of school	Number of males	Number of females	Total male and female
St. Cecelia's Elementary School	13	27	40
Iras Elementary School	20	12	32
Söpwüük Elementary School	19	12	31
Moen Junior High School	3	8	11
Truk High School	0	11	11
Adult Education Program (High School Equivalency)	3	0	3
TOTAL	58	70	128

Source: Author's field notes.

reflected in the next largest group of students who attend Iras Elementary School next door to the Truk District Legislature building. An almost equal number of elementary schoolers hike through Peniya and up a shortcut past Xavier High School to reach Söpwüük Elementary School. When the two dozen junior high and high school students from Peniyesene are added to those pupils attending Iras Elementary School, almost half of all Peniyesene students go downtown to school. The number of pupils who leave the village each day for classes constitutes 60 percent of all persons between 5 and 24 years of age in the resident population (see table 2).

Approximately one half of all school-age boys are not in school, whereas 70 percent of their female counterparts are enrolled. Boys are much less likely than girls to be enrolled in school between the ages of 5

TABLE 2
Enrollment Status of School-Age Members of the Peniyesene Resident Population, March 1976

Age cohort	Total persons in age cohort	Number of males		Number of females	
		Enrolled	Not enrolled	Enrolled	Not enrolled
5–9	56	11	23	15	7
10–14	67	34	7	24	2
15–19	47	10	7	26	4
20–24	45	3	20	5	17
TOTAL	215	58	57	70	30

Source: Author's field notes.

and 9 and, beginning with age 15 and extending through age 24, many more boys drop out of school than girls. Table 2 shows that only one third of the young men between the ages of 15 and 24 are in school, while 60 percent of the young women in this age group are enrolled. This discrepancy shows up in its most striking form in table 1 where one discovers that no young man from Peniyesene was enrolled in a regular high school during the 1975–1976 academic year.[5] A major reason for this is that many young men are expelled from junior high or high school for drinking alcohol and subsequently causing trouble.

Along with the students, a sizable number of adults join the daily exodus from the village to work in the wage economy (table 3). Almost one half of all males over age 15 are employed, although less than 15 percent of all females in this age group work for wages. Table 3 shows that all but four men between the ages of 30 and 50 and just over one half of all men over 30 commute daily to wage jobs. Among young men between 15 and 29 years of age, however, a heavy majority (nearly three fourths) is unemployed. The implications of this for drunken behavior by young men is assessed in later chapters.

Summing students and workers together, 207 persons leave Peniyesene every weekday morning to pursue education or a career outside the village. This means that 44 percent of the entire village population is gone for most of every day (table 4). When the number of nonstudents and nonworkers who venture into town to shop, to seek medical attention at the hospital, to visit friends or relatives, or to transact other business is added to this figure, at least one half of the village of Peniyesene is involved in this daily migration.

A number of other features of Peniyesene life are reminiscent of American suburbia. Among the more well-to-do families in the commu-

TABLE 3
Distribution of Wage Employment in the Peniyesene Resident Population, March 1976

Age cohort	Total persons in age cohort	Number of males			Number of females		
		Employed	Unemployed	Percentage employed	Employed	Unemployed	Percentage employed
15–19	47	2	15	12.5	0	30	9.5
20–24	45	3	20		5	17	
25–29	35[a]	12	10	63	6	7	26
30–34	19[a]	5	0		1	13	
35–39	28	16	1	87.5	4	7	28.5
40–44	17	5	2		2	8	
45–49	15	8	1	75	0	6	0
50–54	12	4	3		0	5	
55–59	17	3	2	38	0	12	0
60–64	14	2	6		0	6	
65+	15	1[b]	7	11	0	7	0
n.s.[c]	1[d]	0	1		0	0	
TOTAL	265[a]	61	68	47	18	118[e]	13

Source: Author's field notes.

[a]Figures exclude the Americans enumerated in the Peniyesene resident population (see table 4).

[b]This man was a member of the Truk District Land Commission, which hears land disputes in connection with the Trust Territory's Cadastral Survey Project.

[c]n.s. = not stated.

[d]This individual is known to be at least 50 years old.

[e]Although most women were not directly employed in the wage economy, most of the women who were married at census time (N=64/118) were married to men employed for wages (N=41/64).

22

nity, a nice lawn has become something of a status symbol, and older members of these families can be seen outside weeding and tending ornamental plants. One of the favorite pastimes of young men from the village is to joyride about the island in a taxi or sedan, often imbibing in the process. Those who do not have a vehicle at their disposal for joyriding hang out in the vicinity of the bridge and the poolhall "watching all the girls go by" and flirting whenever the opportunity arises (figure 12). Among employed males over age 30, many participate in a tavern culture quite like that described by LeMasters (1975) for blue-collar American workers, with the important exception that their wives are not included. Since these men are absent from the village all day while at their jobs, their evening exodus to the bars means that they spend almost no time with their wives and children.

TABLE 4
Demographic Profile of Peniyesene Resident Population, March 1976

Age cohort	Number of males	Number of females	Total male and female
0–4	35	46	81
5–9	34	22	56
10–14	41	26	67
15–19	17	30	47
20–24	23	22	45
25–29	24	15	39
30–34	6	15	21
35–39	17	11	28
40–44	7	10	17
45–49	9	6	15
50–54	7	5	12
55–59	5	12	17
60–64	8	6	14
65+	8	7	15
n.s.[a]	1[b]	0	1
TOTAL	242	233	475[c]

Source: Author's field notes.
Note: The resident population, as here defined, includes all persons who resided in the community for at least one week during the month of March 1976 (see also footnote 8).
[a]n.s. = not stated.
[b]This individual is known to be at least 50 years old.
[c]Includes seven resident Americans: one male, 30–34; one female, 30–34; two males, 25–29; two females, 25–29; one male, 0–4.

Figure 12. View from the bridge over the Wiichen River of
Peniyesene village along the road to downtown

PENIYESENE: HISTORICAL BACKGROUND

Informants disagree on how long Peniyesene has existed as a separate
district of Moen. Some assert that it has great antiquity as revealed by its
mention in the ancient secret language of *itang* 'religious-magical-military experts.' Others—principally those from Peniya or Tunnuuk—claim
that Peniyesene is a fairly recent creation that hived off from its immediate neighbors some time within the last century. Whatever the case, it
is agreed that the community was founded by the stalwart warriors of
Wenikar clan who soundly defeated opponents from Peniya and Tunnuuk
in battle and laid claim to the lands that now comprise Peniyesene. Wenikar was soon joined by members of Sör clan. Through marriage and other
ties additional clans later settled in the community. Today, *chon Peniyesene* 'the people of Peniyesene' belong to nine different clans. They own
the entire peninsula of Wupweyin, the lands along the southern side of
the bay, most of the river valley extending all the way up to and including
Mt. Winifëwürëër,[6] and some of the lands along the ridges above the valley floor.

The clans Wenikar and Sör are widely represented in the Mortlock
Islands to the southeast of Truk, and this has led to numerous ties between
the two areas. Wenikar is the dominant clan on Namoluk Atoll, and it
plays an important role on Nama, Oneop, Etal, and Kutu as well. At least
one Namoluk Wenikar subclan traces its origin to Peniyesene, and over

the years quite a number of Peniyesene-Mortlock marriages have occurred. Deriving from these kinship connections, Peniyesene continues to serve as a home away from home for many Mortlock visitors to Truk.

The once dominant position Wenikar clan held politically and numerically in Peniyesene has been eclipsed by other clans in recent years (see table 5). Although Sör has remained strong, Fenimei, Maasalö, and Wiitä have all overtaken Wenikar. Differential mortality among the clans, attributable to serendipity in childhood deaths and a lack of fertile Wenikar women, primarily accounts for this change.

TABLE 5
Clan Composition of Peniyesene Resident Population, March 1976

Clan name	Number of males	Number of females	Total male and female
Sör	44	41	85
Fenimei	36	46	82
Maasalö	37	33	70
Wiitä	33	29	62
Wenikar	26	20	46
Inänofot	17	27	44
Söpwunipi	16	12	28
Wisusu	8	13	21
Achau	3	1	4
Other[a]	18	8	26
TOTAL	238	230	468[b]

Source: Author's field notes.

[a]The breakdown of other clans is as follows: Souyefang 6 (4 male, 2 female); Fesinim 5 (2 male, 3 female); Pwe 4 (3 male, 1 female); Alangaitau 3 (3 male, 0 female); Wun 2 (0 male, 2 female); Souwon 2 (2 male, 0 female); Soumöch 1 (1 male, 0 female); Pukos 1 (1 male, 0 female); Lewel 1 (1 male, 0 female); Leafö 1 (1 male, 0 female). None of these clans was established in Peniyesene in March 1976.

[b]Figure does not include the seven Americans resident in the community, who, despite intensive interrogation by the ethnographer, could not be coaxed into revealing their clan identities.

Several Japanese men moved into Peniyesene during the 1930s, married Peniyesene women, and fathered children who have remained in the community. During World War II large numbers of Japanese soldiers were sent to Truk, and Peniyesene became a major billet for army troops. Barracks were built, fortifications were installed, air raid shelters were blasted into the basalt bedrock along the valley's edges,[7] and as the war progressed, gardens were appropriated and the population of Peniyesene was removed, some to Wütëët Island and others to the back side of Mt. Wiitipwen. The Japanese troop concentration made the village a prime target for American bombers late in the war. Several Peniyesene persons were killed in the bombings, others sustained injuries, and most families lost their belongings and homes.

Few censuses have been taken that specifically enumerate the residents of Peniyesene apart from the rest of Moen, but the data we possess make it clear that Peniyesene's population, like that of the entire port town island, has exploded in the post-World War II period. The Japanese census of 1930 counted 172 persons in Peniyesene, and this number declined to 154 by the time of the 1935 census (Japan 1931c, 1937). My census, taken in March 1976, found 475 persons residing in the village, almost exactly three times the 1935 figure (see table 4).[8]

PENIYESENE: THE CONTEMPORARY SOCIAL SETTING

In most major respects Peniyesene social organization follows that described by Goodenough (1951) for Romónum Island in Truk Lagoon.[9] Peniyesene's clans consist of localized matrilineages, which in some cases are organized into subclans. Most married couples reside with the wife's relatives in an extended family arrangement. Three or sometimes four generations live together in adjacent dwellings and eat out of a common hearth. Nearly every Peniyesene resident continues to consume some local foods grown on individually owned, or lineage, lands, in addition to the imported rice, flour, bread, canned fish, and frozen meat that form part of the regular diet. Primary loyalties are to one's matrikin and close created kinsmen, particularly to those in the same lineage. Beyond this, a more diffuse loyalty is felt to others from Peniyesene itself. These lineage and district loyalties are important in understanding many of the fights that frequently erupt among young men who have been drinking.

Peniyesene's resident population contains numerous immigrants from other communities in Truk District (table 6). Even so, for a suburb of a modern Micronesian port town, Peniyesene has retained a remarkable homogeneity in the composition of its population when compared with a downtown village such as Iras. Better than two thirds of Peniyesene's resident population in March 1976 belonged to established village lineages. Reflecting its historical ties with the Mortlocks, the greatest number of immigrants from outside Truk Lagoon in the Peniyesene population came from this region.

While its resident population has remained relatively intact, little else distinguishes Peniyesene as a distinct entity. For practical purposes there are no village elected officials such as are found in most other communities in Truk District. No one is generally recognized as village magistrate; no village council meets; no records of births, deaths, marriages, and the like are kept by a village secretary; and no local police enforce village regulations and help keep the peace. All these political functions

TABLE 6
Communities of Origin for Members of the Peniyesene Resident Population,
March 1976

Island/ community	Number of persons	
	Subtotal	Total
Islands in Truk Lagoon		425
Moen	395[a]	
Wuumaan	5	
Paata	5	
Piis-Moen	5	
Dublon	5	
Toon	3	
Wütëët	2	
Fano	2	
Feefen	1	
Parem	1	
Romonum	1	
Islands in the Mortlocks		31
Namoluk Atoll	12	
Nama Island	6	
Oncop, Lukunor Atoll	5	
Losap, Losap Atoll	4	
Piis-Losap, Losap Atoll	2	
Möch, Satawan Atoll	1	
Kutu, Satawan Atoll	1	
Islands in the Halls, Westerns, and Namonuito		11
Fananu, Nomwin Atoll	5	
Puluwat Atoll	4	
Pisarach, Namonuito Atoll	1	
Murilö, Murilö Atoll	1	
Islands elsewhere in Micronesia		1
Ponape Island	1[b]	
Countries outside Micronesia		7
United States	7	
TOTAL		475

Source: Author's field notes.

[a]This figure breaks down by village/district as follows: Peniyesene—325; Peniya—39; Tunnuuk—26; Iras—2; Söpwüuk—1; Mecchitiw—1; Mwään—1.

[b]From the Mortlock community on Ponape.

have been given over to the Moen municipal government, which holds sway over the entire port town island. Although Peniyesene elects a representative to the Moen Municipal Council, the net result of the general abdication of village autonomy has been to create a vacuum in place of any sense of political community that once existed. This vacuum has led to a kind of minimal investment by most residents in internal village affairs. The village takes on an air of lawlessness during the frequent fighting conducted by local drunks.

Visitors in Peniyesene are made up of friends and relatives from all over Truk District. Some stay only a day or two, perhaps while seeing a doctor at the hospital, and then return home to Toon or Wuumaan. Others may reside in the community for a month or more while awaiting the next ship that will return them to their outer island home. Still others move in for extended periods.

A number of the temporary residents in Peniyesene are young, unmarried, unemployed males from other parts of Greater Trukese Society.[10] These young men come into the village via created sibling relationships with Peniyesene young men (Marshall, 1977). They quickly become familiar figures to everyone in the village—especially if they take part in the drunken carousing that plays such an integral role in village life. A few of these outsiders become permanent members of the Peniyesene population by marrying local women and settling down in the community.

Peniyesene is divided approximately equally between Catholics and Protestants. Village Catholics, who make up 45 percent of the population, hold some of their religious services in a newly constructed boathouse in Peniyesene, but for most of their needs they must journey to the Catholic mission station in Tunnuuk. Most Protestants, who comprise 52 percent of the population, attend the church located in the village; however, a few with strong kin connections in Peniya or Tunnuuk attend church in these villages. Two Peniyesene persons are Jehovah's Witnesses, two claim to be agnostics, and the religious affiliations of seven persons remain unknown.

Most wage earners (two thirds) in Peniyesene are employed in government jobs rather than in the private sector (table 7). This reflects both the better wages to be had from government jobs and the fact that the private sector is relatively undeveloped in Micronesia today.

Substantial differences in monetary and material wealth exist among Peniyesene's population, as evidenced in everything from housing to transportation to clothing and diet. Some residents are, by Micronesian standards, rich; others are abysmally poor. Considerable evidence exists that these differences in wealth are giving rise to emergent social classes. Some residents of Peniyesene own two cars and live in new cement homes with linoleum floors, glass louvred windows, kerosene refrigerators or freezers, western-style furniture, and electricity (from small diesel generators), which is used to run electric lights, fans, and, in at least one case, a washing machine. These same wealthy families operate one or two motorboats equipped with 25 horsepower Johnson or Evinrude outboard engines, dress in stylish clothing, purchase fancy toys for their children, and

TABLE 7
Jobs Held by Members of the Peniyesene Resident Population, March 1976

Employment in the private sector			Employment in the public sector		
Job classification	Number of men	Number of women	Job classification	Number of men	Number of women
Construction laborer	5	0	Public works[a]	12	0
Store clerk/worker	3	2	Education	10[b]	0
Taxi driver	3	0	Hospital[c]	4	5
Cook	1	2	Public health	2	0
Bank clerk/teller	1	1	Sanitation	1	0
Business office worker	0	2	District administrator's		
Waitress	0	2	office[d]	1	1
Self-employed	2[f]	0	District legislator	1[e]	0
Commercial			Clerk of the court	1	0
fisherman	1	0	Finance	0	1[g]
Automobile mechanic	1	0	Supply	1	0
Teacher (St. Cecelia's)	1	0	Agriculture	1[h]	0
Laundress	0	1	Housing Authority	1[i]	0
			Labor	1	0
			Community development	1	0
			Land Commission	1	0
			Communication station	1[j]	0
			Radio announcer, WSZC	0	1
			U.S. Weather Station	1[k]	0
			Foreman, Ferrocement		
			boatbuilding project	1	0
			Janitor, courthouse	1	0
			CETA Youth Corps		
			trainee	1	0
TOTAL	18	10		43	8

Source: Author's field notes.

[a]Includes employees in the following categories: electrician, mechanic, heavy equipment operator, carpenter, telephone operator, body andfender repairman, boat repairman, and assistant inspector.

[b]Includes two teachers at Moen Junior High School, four at Söpwüük Elementary School, two attending a special teacher training program at Iras Elementary School, the Truk High School cook, and a boat operator and handyman.

[c]Includes employees in the following categories: nurse, health aide, dental assistant, cashier, night watchman, operating room assistant, and X-ray technician.

[d]Includes the driver for the district administrator and the secretary to the deputy district administrator.

[e]Representing Namoluk Atoll. This man is married to a Peniyesene woman and resides in the village.

[f]One as a boatbuilder and one as a taxi owner and small-scale commercial fisherman.

[g]Clerk-accountant.

[h]This man is the agricultural extension agent on Namoluk Atoll. He was temporarily resident in Peniyesene at census time, having come to Moen for treatment of an injury at the hospital.

[i]Truk District housing inspector. This man also owns the cafe-poolhall in Peniyesene and operates a taxi driven by his wife's brother.

[j]Electronics technician.

[k]Meteorological technician.

diaper their babies with disposable diapers. Family meals regularly include frozen Australian beef, chicken from the United States, and such delicacies as cinnamon rolls flown in fresh on Air Mike from Tommy's Bakery on Guam.

At the other end of the village economic scale, several large families have no member employed for wages and continue to subsist on a traditional Trukese diet of breadfruit, taro, and fresh fish, supplemented by small amounts of imported food, such as rice and flour. Their minimal monetary resources derive from the sale of copra to the TTC or from occasional part-time labor for wealthier members of the community. They own neither car nor motorboat and are lucky to own a canoe. Their homes are either single-room plywood boxes or small structures made piecemeal from corrugated tin, old packing crates, and random pieces of lumber. Their clothing is old and tattered and their children have no fine toys with which to amuse themselves.

These large differences in wealth and life-style are galling to many Trukese who hold egalitarianism as a fundamental ethic; the drunken behavior of many young men in the community is not unrelated to perceived class differences. Several of the wealthier individuals in Peniyesene keep .22 caliber rifles to deal with persons who might try to break into their homes at night.

This, then, is the setting for our investigation. We will focus on the consumption of alcoholic beverages by members of the Peniyesene community, particularly young men between the ages of 18 and 35, some of whom may drink downtown and then return to Peniyesene to participate in the recurrent drama of *chon sakau* 'the village drunks. On rare occasions this drama becomes a "game of death," which rivals that engaged in by Bruce Lee on the local movie screen.

The Evolution
of Trukese Drinking

2

These [islands of Truk] are inhabited by some ten
thousand natives, not by nature indocile, but broken
into hostile clans, and of dangerous repute with the
traders and whalers who have hitherto avoided them.

Reverend S. E. Bishop,
"Missionary life of Mr. Logan"

MICRONESIA'S CONTACT WITH THE OUTSIDE WORLD

After Magellan and his crew put in at Guam on their pioneering circum-
navigation of the globe in 1521, it took another three centuries before most
of Micronesia was discovered and explored by the West. The scattered
exploratory probes that followed Magellan's during the sixteenth and sev-
enteenth centuries led to the establishment of a Spanish colony in the
Marianas in 1668, centered on Guam, to service the annual Manila galleon
sailing to Acapulco. Largely on the basis of their priority in the Marianas,
the Spaniards claimed suzerainty over the Carolines and Marshalls as
well, although they undertook no colonization of these islands. Explorers
representing other European nations also ventured into Micronesian waters
during this early period, but in most cases their contacts were of brief
duration and were not followed up by attempts at administrative control.

Truk's first known contact with the West was with the Spanish ship
San Lucas in 1565, captained by Alonso de Arellano (Hezel 1973b). Following this early contact, Truk was not again visited by Europeans for

two and one-half centuries until Manuel Dublon called aboard the brig *San Antonio* in December 1814.

Although the rough geographical outline of Micronesia was known to the West by the early eighteenth century, it was to be at least another 100 years before this outline was completely filled in. Many islands in Micronesia were discovered by the whalers and traders who began to frequent these waters late in the eighteenth and early nineteenth centuries as the on-the-line whaling grounds were opened up. Also during this era of increasing contact, the first beachcomber colonies sprang up on the high islands of Ponape and Kosrae.

With the beachcombers and whalers came the introduction of all sorts of novel things from muskets and rum to new genes and new ideas. It was a time of turmoil for many Micronesians. It was also a period where no outside power exercised effective jurisdiction anywhere outside the Marianas, the Spanish claim notwithstanding. By the time Protestant missionaries first arrived from Hawaii in 1852, patterns of interaction with and expectations about foreigners were already firmly established on many islands.

The major whaling grounds of the western Pacific began to shift northward from Micronesian waters near the equator to the off-Japan grounds by the mid-nineteenth century, although the whaleships still had recourse to such ports of call as Ponape and Guam for replenishments. More or less coincident with this change, resident traders began moving into the islands of Micronesia. Many such men were independent traders who differed little from the beachcombers of earlier years. Others, however, were in the employ of large commercial firms headquartered in such cities as Hamburg, Auckland, or Honolulu. Micronesians began to make copra and dry *bêche-de-mer* in exchange for a wide variety of trade goods, including firearms and alcoholic beverages.

In eastern Micronesia, the Protestant missionaries waged a continuous battle during the last half of the nineteenth century with beachcombers, whalers, and traders for the hearts and souls of Micronesians. At issue was a whole style of life and set of values that would be imparted to the islanders, although much of the acrimony between the two groups centered on trade, particularly on traffic in "ardent spirits" (Marshall and Marshall 1976). Although the Protestant mission was extremely influential in shaping Micronesian attitudes toward outsiders, and although the Protestant church remains today one of the most viable institutions in Micronesia, the American missionaries eventually lost out to a combination of German mercantilism and colonialism.

Recognizing that Spain's strength as an international power was declining, Germany began challenging the Spanish claim to hegemony in the Marshalls and Carolines in the 1870s and 1880s. In 1885, the German government directly defied Spain by formally annexing the Marshall Islands and attempted to occupy the Carolines. This latter move was thwarted only by papal arbitration, but German trading posts were allowed to remain on all the important islands of the Carolines (Firth 1973). In 1899, following Spain's defeat in the Spanish-American War (Brown 1976), her rights to the Carolines eventually were purchased by Germany. At this same time, the island of Guam came under American control.

The Spanish period in the Carolines, usually dated from 1885 to 1899, was succeeded briefly by German administrative control from 1899 to 1914. The Germans, much more industrious than the Spaniards in taking hold of the islands, lost little time in setting up copra plantations and exploiting the rich phosphate deposits on Nauru (which Germany annexed in 1888) and Angaur. German influence became so strong during this time that the missionaries of the American Board of Commissioners for Foreign Missions (ABCFM) handed the field over to the German Liebenzell mission in 1907. The Liebenzell missionaries did not alter the firm stance taken by the ABCFM against alcohol and tobacco, as is evident in the following statement that appeared in the *Missionary Herald:*

> Knowing the views of the native Christians of these islands in reference to the use of narcotics and intoxicants, which have a specially deleterious effect upon these islanders, the question naturally occurred as to what views were entertained by these German recruits. In correspondence with Pastor Blecker inquiry was made upon this point, and he replies in behalf of the German Christian Endeavorers: "It is a great pleasure to me to tell you that it would be always a chief condition for all our missionaries not to use tobacco or intoxicants. We do not consider it as respectable in our circles to use such things." [*MH* 1906: 576]

The American missionaries' legacy of staunch opposition to alcohol and tobacco lived on.[1]

Although the German period in Micronesia was of rather brief duration, it was revolutionary in its consequences for the islanders, "for it meant access to European technology, loss of traditional lands, recruitment as labourers and subjection to foreign rule" (Firth 1973:28). The brevity of German administrative control in Micronesia was a direct consequence of her entry into World War I. Germany could no longer afford to defend her island possessions in the Pacific, and Micronesia fell quickly and bloodlessly to the newly modernized Japanese Navy in October 1914. Thus was born Micronesia's third colonial experience in less than thirty years.

Japanese control of Micronesia was made official in 1921 when the islands were designated a Class C mandate by the League of Nations; the area was controlled as such until the end of World War II. It was during the Japanese period that profound social and cultural changes swept over most of Micronesia, although we still know little about this period of

Micronesian history. One fact that emerges with great clarity from this era, however, is that the Japanese continued and expanded the German effort to exploit the area economically (Purcell 1976). Commercial agriculture and fishing were begun on a large scale; public works and communication and transportation facilities were constructed; a wage-work economy grew up; Micronesians were provided with an elementary education; and large-scale immigration of Japanese nationals to the islands took place. The benefits to Micronesians from such modernization, however, were "the secondary results of the South Seas Bureau's concern with utilizing the islands in the best interests of the Japanese" (Purcell 1976:211).

One of those interests was military expansion. Japanese fortification of the islands of Micronesia began in the late 1930s, and large numbers of military personnel were moved into the area during World War II. Several major amphibious battles were fought on the Micronesian islands of Peleliu, Guam, and Saipan, and many other islands were heavily bombarded by the Allied military. Truk, which was a major Japanese naval base, was surprised in an aerial attack in February 1944, and bombing raids continued there for nearly the duration of the war. Many Micronesians lost their lives, loved ones, and possessions during World War II, which remains a bitter memory only now beginning to fade.

With the Japanese surrender aboard the battleship *Missouri* in Tokyo Bay, the U. S. Navy assumed control of Micronesia. Echoing the chain of events following World War I, the United Nations awarded America a strategic trusteeship over the Caroline, Marshall, and Mariana Islands. Guam, lost at the outbreak of the war, reverted to territorial status under the United States, separate from the U. S. Trust Territory of the Pacific Islands. The Navy ruled Micronesia from 1945 until 1951, when a civil administration under jurisdiction of the Department of the Interior was established. With small modification, this system of administration endures to the present.

The Navy faced the task of trying to set Micronesia's shattered economy back on its feet. Numerous studies were carried out to this end, and the U. S. Commercial Company was set up in an effort to get things moving. Economic growth languished until the early 1960s, however, when the U. S. Congress began to allocate large sums of money for the Trust Territory budget. The budget grew more than tenfold from $7.4 million in 1961 to $80.0 million in 1974, and this rapid infusion of money bred as many problems as it solved. Unquestionably, most Micronesians today enjoy a material standard of living higher than any ever seen in the islands before, but many Micronesians feel as if they have sold their souls to the devil. Much of this money has gone for programs and salaries that do not contribute to meaningful economic development. At least one observer feels that American giveaway programs and education have fostered "a strange and dangerous sense of unreality" in the islands (Nevin 1977).

34

One of the major social problems in the Trust Territory, pointed to by Micronesians and Americans alike, is alcohol abuse.[2] The history of alcoholic beverages in Truk District is presented in the paragraphs that follow, in part to dispel some of the myths about Trukese drunken comportment, and in part to delineate the continuity in the ways Trukese have used alcoholic beverages over the past eighty or ninety years.

MEETING DEMON RUM

Like most of North America, the islands of Oceania lacked alcoholic beverages of any sort at first contact with the West. In both areas, however, Europeans lost no time in introducing the native peoples to the pleasures and problems of alcohol. Alcoholic beverages were offered first by explorers as a sign of friendship and hospitality, and liquor later became an integral part of trade. Although firewater soon came to rank next to firearms as a trade item eagerly sought by Indians and Pacific Islanders, it was initially rejected by the indigenes. Only after they had had numerous opportunities to observe the bizarre changes alcohol wrought in the behavior of their European and American visitors, did the indigenes become intrigued enough to taste again. When they did drink, they modeled their behavior after the drunken mayhem of the foreigners who brought alcohol among them (see MacAndrew and Edgerton 1969 and Marshall and Marshall 1976 for examples).

In the case of Pacific Islanders, the most influential of these foreigners were the crews of whaleships and beachcombers. Even when sober, the whaling crews were unrestrained in behavior, and the release that accompanied "shore leave" after being cooped up aboard ship for months on end was often explosive. Brawling and boisterous carousing were the inevitable accompaniment of the drinking engaged in by these men on the Pacific Islands. Resident beachcombers not only provided the islanders with examples of raucous and belligerent drunken comportment but in many cases taught them how to manufacture their own fermented and distilled alcoholic beverages. Everything from bananas and oranges to coconut sap to the sugary root of *Cordyline fruticosa* was tested and turned into "the water that takes away one's wits."

The peoples of Oceania lacked alcoholic beverages but many used other drug substances. The most common of these were obtained from two related plants: kava, an infusion made from the pounded root of *Piper methysticum*, and betel, the fresh leaves of *Piper betle*, which are chewed in a quid with powdered lime and the fragrant seed of the *Areca* palm. Generally speaking, where betel was chewed, kava was not drunk, and vice versa. Neither substance was found universally over the Pacific region. Kava consumption had its greatest elaboration in the formal kava ceremonies of Western Polynesia, but it was used throughout most of Polynesia and in much of Melanesia and New Guinea. In Micronesia, however, kava was made only on the two high islands of Ponape and Kosrae in the eastern Carolines. Betel was chewed in wide areas of Melanesia and New Guinea and in the islands of Yap, Palau, and the Marianas in Micronesia.

Unlike many other Pacific Islanders, the people of Truk had no indigenous drug substance like kava or betel that was consumed ritually or recreationally. Trukese possessed a considerable herbal pharmacopia for the treatment of illness and injury, but they represented one of the world's few cultures that lacked a traditional, widely consumed drug substance like caffeine, nicotine, kava, or ethanol. Although they were aware of kava from canoe visits to Ponape, and although *Piper methysticum* grows on some of the high islands of Truk Lagoon, people in Greater Trukese Society never made kava.

This lack of experience with drugs did not prevent Trukese from avidly seeking tobacco early in the contact period. The date at which tobacco first reached Truk is unknown, but, like many other Pacific Islanders, the Trukese seemed willing to do almost anything to obtain it. This weakness was of course exploited by the traders who eventually moved into the area.[3] The first trader to take up residence in the Mortlocks (in 1872) described the natives of Ta Islet in Satawan Atoll as honest and reported that nothing was stolen from him during his seven-month residence there except four and one-half sticks of tobacco (Wawn n.d.). Five years later, John Westwood settled down on Lukunor Islet in Lukunor Atoll to trade for the firm of Henderson and MacFarlane, and he regularly purchased up to twenty coconuts (used to make copra) "for a paltry stick of Niggerhead tobacco." According to Westwood (1905:101), "smoking is one of their weaknesses and the sale of tobacco to them is one of the most profitable businesses."

If smoking was a weakness of the Mortlock Islanders (and, presumably, of the Lagoon Trukese as well) in the late 1870s, by the early part of the twentieth century they were hopelessly addicted. Bollig says that Trukese held smoking "dearer than food and drink," and that

> there is scarcely anything in Truk for which one will be so adored
> as tobacco. For some, no price for tobacco is too high. A gift of
> tobacco makes happy countenances among chiefs and
> subordinates. If the people are apathetic from hunger or heat, the
> little words *un egis suwa* 'here is some tobacco' reinvigorate them.
> [1927:165; translation by Leslie B. Marshall]

This passionate desire for tobacco collided squarely with the ascetic teachings of the Protestant missionaries of the ABCFM. These persons moved into the Mortlocks in the early 1870s and established a station in Truk Lagoon in 1879, manned by a Ponapean Christian who was joined in 1884 by Reverend Robert Logan and his wife. Reverend Logan quickly made clear to the Trukese that Christians were different from other foreigners in that they did not smoke. Giving up tobacco became the symbol of taking on Christianity early in the mission period (Marshall and Marshall 1976). What is surprising is not that the missionaries of the ABCFM opposed tobacco use, for they had a long tradition of such opposition elsewhere in the Pacific,[4] but rather that in Greater Trukese Society the missionaries encountered a people as yet "uncontaminated" by alcoholic beverages. This was clearly a consequence of Truk's widespread reputation as "Dread Hogoleu,"[5] which served to keep foreigners away for much of the nineteenth century.

Ponape and Kosrae were favorite beachcomber haunts and ports of call for whalers. Both islands were introduced to alcoholic beverages by westerners in the 1830s and 1840s. By the time the ABCFM arrived in 1852, the manufacture and use of alcohol was well known and widespread. Thus it is all the more startling that Truk and the surrounding atolls had no alcohol as late as 1888.

Visiting the mission station in Truk in 1880, the Reverend E. T. Doane wrote with obvious elation that the Trukese eye was "round, black and lustrous, not dimmed by the use of ava or toddy from the cocoanut blossom" (1881:209). Upon settling among the Trukese four years later, the Reverend Robert Logan confirmed this observation, noting that "they make no use whatever of anything intoxicating" (1886:16). Elaborating on this, Logan said,

> the people are utterly without intoxicants of any kind. Toddy, from cocoa-sap, is very easily made; but the people throw it away when it ferments, thinking it spoiled. This seems strange, as they will eat fish after they smell so badly as nearly to knock one over. Doubtless white men will some time teach them to drink, as they have at the Marshall Is.; but at any rate the gospel is here first. [1886:18]

Despite Logan's prediction that the introduction of alcoholic beverages was just a matter of time, another ABCFM missionary reported in 1888 that "no intoxicating drinks are used. A wicked trader who wished to injure our work offered the natives liquor to make them drunk, and when drunk they were to come and do wicked things. The whole scheme failed, as the natives quickly rejected the liquor, saying it burnt their mouths" (Treiber 1888:325–326).

Given the fervency with which Protestant missionaries in eastern Micronesia opposed alcohol use, it is impossible to imagine them failing to comment on alcoholic beverages were they present. From the first missionary visit to the Mortlocks in late 1872, up through at least 1905, use of alcoholic beverages in the Mortlocks is never mentioned in the extensive missionary literature. The absence of alcohol in the Mortlocks during this period is further supported by the accounts of the traders Wawn and Westwood, neither of whom mentions natives consuming or manufacturing liquor. Since both the missionaries and the traders specifically comment on other vices, such as tobacco and tumeric body paint, alcohol becomes conspicuous by its absence. The first ethnographer of Namoluk Atoll in the Mortlocks, who conducted research there sometime during the first decade of this century, mentioned that "the making of palm wine [coconut toddy] is unknown," and noted that "debauchery does not occur, which is assured by the lack of any intoxicating beverages" (Girschner 1912:140, 209; translation by Dianne Maughan).

While the Trukese lacked alcoholic beverages early in the contact period, they certainly did not lack audacity in dealing with foreigners. Beginning in the mid-sixteenth century and continuing through the mid-nineteenth century, the Trukese boldly attacked nearly every European ship that happened into their lagoon (Hezel 1973a, 1973b). Even so, Hezel is correct in stressing that a notorious reputation by itself is insufficient reason to account for whalers shunning Truk, particularly when the evidence indicates that many other Micronesians dealt with foreign vessels just as directly. But if Truk offered fewer inducements to visiting whaleships than Ponape and Kosrae on account of its relative paucity of fresh water, diversified crops, and willing women (Hezel 1973a), the fact remains that Truk's warlike reputation did retard the more insidious forms of contact that occurred elsewhere.

More than anyone else, Andrew Cheyne succeeded in publicizing Truk's reputation for treachery and bellicosity. Nearly cut off there in October 1844 while gathering bêche-de-mer, Cheyne later published a stern warning about Truk that received wide publicity: "No vessel should visit this group . . . unless well-manned and armed, as the natives . . . will be certain to attack any vessel which they may find in a defenseless state" (1852:56). It is important to realize, however, that the Trukese did not attack only the outsiders who came into their midst; they were constantly engaged in interdistrict and interisland skirmishing. Hezel attributes the long delay in extensive outside contact primarily to this incessant fighting, which discouraged traders and others from moving into the area for reasons of personal safety. The factionalism and shifting alliances that characterized Trukese traditional warfare meant that foreigners ran a constant risk of becoming identified with a particular group and thence of becoming fair game for this group's enemies. Indeed, it is this phenomenon that seems to account for the deaths of at least three traders who lived in Truk after 1880 (Hezel 1973a).

By the early 1890s traders began to peddle their familiar combination of firearms and firewater in Truk, even though the former far outweighed the latter in initial popularity. An extract from a missionary journal laments:

> Our neighbors at Ruk [Truk] see trouble ahead. A trader has announced that he is going to bring guns to all the Ruk Islands. The German traders at Ruk say they shall do the same. The natives are so eager to get guns, tobacco and whiskey that they would not hesitate to sell their food for them; and many of them would sell their souls as well. . . . [Pease 1893:15]

This is probably a reference to the decision by Japanese traders, who first came into Truk in the 1890s, to sell guns to compete with the Germans and other traders who had moved into the area in the previous decade. The Japanese trading companies sold liquor along with rifles and ammunition. This combination, coupled with the effective competition the Japanese provided, led the German administration to close down the Japanese trading companies in 1899 (Purcell 1971; Yanaihara 1940).

Writing of the period shortly before firearms became widely available to Trukese, the Reverend Robert Logan chronicles a continuing stream of violence in Truk Lagoon. For instance, the people of Mecchitiw district on Moen were "fighting among themselves with guns, spears, and knives" in March 1887, and shortly after they were at it again (ABCFM 1888:20, 23). Logan also discusses the "shameful murders" soon thereafter of some Hall Islanders by warriors from Tunnuuk district on Moen in revenge for the death of one of their young men who had been visiting in the Halls (ABCFM 1888:23–24). A smoldering feud between Kuku and Sapore districts on Feefen received comment when it flared into open fighting, and an encounter involving men from Dublon is described in which five men were killed (ABCFM 1888:33, 37). That such fighting was not restricted to islanders in Truk Lagoon is made clear by Logan when he mentions church members on Kutu Islet, Satawan Atoll, fighting each other with knives and spears, severely wounding several persons (ABCFM 1888:9). Somewhat ironically, most of the medical work engaged in by the Logans as messengers of peace involved caring for wounds resulting from minor fights and feuds (Aberley 1975:41).

The introduction of lots of firearms to Truk in the 1890s exacerbated traditional warfare by making it a new and more deadly game. It also meant that the Trukese posed a much greater potential threat to foreigners. Given the stubborn opposition to Spanish and German rule on Ponape, where armed rebellions broke out against each of these colonial governments, the reasons why the feared warriors of Truk disarmed so peacefully in 1904 have long fascinated scholars working in Micronesia. Various hypotheses have been put forth to explain this apparent anomaly, including the nature of Trukese personality (Swartz 1965); the fact that disarmament offered a resolution of traditional warfare that had rather suddenly gotten out of hand on account of the new weapons (Clifton 1964); and the lack of traditional suprafamilial authority that could cope with this new level of aggression (Hezel 1973a). These explanations are interrelated, and they coalesce around the expression and control of aggression. As such, they bear directly on matters of Trukese drunken comportment to be discussed in later chapters.

Although the Germans succeeded in getting Trukese to give up firearms following the edict of 1904, at approximately this same time firewater began to take on a new fascination. As an end was put to traditional warfare, Trukese began to consume alcoholic beverages more frequently. The prohibition on warfare was followed by an upswing in drinking, until a prohibition was put on drinking by the Japanese administration some years later.

The islanders of Greater Trukese Society lacked acquaintance with alcoholic beverages at least as late as 1888,[6] and widespread drinking did not begin until the early twentieth century. But when it began, it did so with a vengeance. Few records from the period between 1905 and 1920 mention alcohol use by Trukese. The fragments of information that do exist reveal that drinking had captured the Trukese imagination almost as much as smoking tobacco had earlier. Bollig describes competitive feasts at which "mountains of food" were gathered and to which the very rich contributed foreign items like rice, biscuit, salmon, beer, and schnapps (1927:82). Bollig says that "in Japanese times, this custom degenerated so much from alcohol use, that many fell *fan tebel*, i.e., 'under the table' and had to be dragged home by their relatives" (1927:184; translation by Leslie B. Marshall).

Manufacture of fermented coconut toddy or palm wine was rare in Truk proper at this time, but Bollig mentions the Puluwat Islanders as well-known toddy drinkers. This echoes Krämer's terse comments on the subject: "Palm wine is not used or at least is used infrequently" (1932:124). Like Bollig, the German anthropologists found the use of fermented toddy to be concentrated in the Western Islands of Truk District (Thilenius and Hellwig 1927:275). LeBar's note that "according to Romónum informants, the Trukese were unaware of the fermentation process until comparatively recently, when they learned it from Puluwat Islanders" (1964:224) shows that while foreigners introduced trade alcohol to the islands of Truk Lagoon, they apparently did not teach the Trukese how to manufacture locally produced alcoholic beverages. This makes sense since there were no beachcombers in Truk; the traders could only damage their own business interests by showing their customers how simple it is to make what had become a much sought after item of trade. Available evidence suggests that the Western Islanders learned sour toddy manufacture from persons on the central Carolinian atolls where this knowledge had diffused from the Spanish colony in the Marianas (Marshall and Marshall 1975). Even though palm wine has a mean alcohol content of only 5 percent (Leong 1953:256), Bollig reports "drunkenness, brawling and manslaughter" to be "the results of its enjoyment" (1927:164). The transition in Truk from fearless warrior to fearsome drunk had already begun.

THE PROHIBITION ERA: 1921–1959

Before the League of Nations bestowed its imprimatur on Japan's control of Micronesia in 1921, heavy use of imported alcoholic beverages had become common at Trukese competitive feasts. With the award of the Japanese mandate, however, the Japanese began to abide by the League of Nations' stipulation that intoxicating liquors be kept from the natives. This international pressure, combined with their own desire to bring order to the region, led the Japanese to promulgate formal regulations for the control of intoxicating liquors beginning on December 1, 1921 (see appendix).[7]

That official prohibition did not dampen the Micronesians' desire for alcoholic beverages can be seen by examining the annual reports made by the Japanese government to the League of Nations. In the report for 1923, under the heading "Trade and Manufacture of Alcohol and Drugs," Micronesians are described as "obedient" persons who "faithfully observe the regulations," and the report concludes that "there is no need of any particular campaign against alcoholism" (Japan 1924:5). But less than a decade later the picture had changed. The annual report for 1930 grudgingly admits a tendency for both Japanese residents and natives to commit an increasing number of crimes from year to year, *"especially conspicuous being an increase in the number of persons infringing the Rules for the Control of Liquors"* (Japan 1931a:15; emphasis added). By this time, breaking the liquor laws was already the most common legal offense in the territory, making up 60 percent of all offenses committed, a figure three times that of theft, the second most common category of crime. Prohibition in Japanese-controlled Micronesia worked no better than it has anywhere else in the world.

Nearly all the alcoholic beverages consumed in Micronesia during the period of the Japanese mandate were either imported from Japan or locally produced. Although limited small-scale individual production had been under way on Saipan for several years, the government granted permission to the Nanyō Kōhatsu Kabushiki Kaisha (South Seas Development Company, Ltd.) in June 1926 to manufacture beverage alcohol as a by-product of the recently founded sugar industry in the Marianas. This commercial venture was supplemented by ten persons who had been licensed to make intoxicating liquors on Saipan by 1928 (Japan 1927, 1929).

41

By 1932, the liquor producers in the Northern Marianas began exporting a small quantity of their goods to Guam, the Dutch Celebes, and the Gilbert Islands, although the bulk of their output continued to go to Japan (Japan 1933). By this time the industry also was producing sake, beer, wine, *shochu*, and whiskey.[8] The year 1932 marked the first official dispensation to persons outside Saipan to manufacture alcoholic beverages. Such permission was granted to one person each in Palau and Truk, at least one of whom was making banana wine.

Violations of the liquor regulations in Truk District accounted for 86 percent of all arrests made during 1937 (U.S. Navy 1944:78). Clearly, the Trukese were obtaining alcoholic beverages despite official prohibition. While some of this liquor undoubtedly was obtained from Japanese bootleggers (U.S. Navy 1944:101), interviews with Trukese persons alive at the time indicate that a great deal of fermented coconut toddy also was being produced.

According to a U. S. Navy report (1944:101), Japanese enforcement of the liquor code in Micronesia grew increasingly lax in the 1930s. Even if this was the case, it seems likely that formal arrests of Trukese for drunkenness represented only a small fraction of the problem. Those caught by Japanese policemen were only those who lived on islands with a substantial Japanese population and who were foolish enough to carouse in public. Many drinkers doubtless went undetected. Informants have told me that regular drinking parties were held on Namoluk Atoll during this period, joined in by the local Okinawan representative of the Japanese government, who often purchased imported alcoholic beverages for the atoll chief. The government is reputed to have tolerated these parties as long as they did not become unduly disruptive. Although it has been charged that the Japanese plied Micronesian chiefs with liquor as a means of making them more amenable to control (U.S. Navy 1944:101), the Namoluk case is a clear instance where the Japanese could not have enforced prohibition even if they had wanted to for a lack of manpower. A similar situation must have obtained elsewhere in the territory, particularly on most outer islands. Then, as now, it must have been easy for a small group of men to slip away undetected into the bush to drink to their hearts' content.

The official Japanese arrest records for liquor violations are important in helping us put similar records from the American period in proper perspective. These latter records often are pointed to as a clear indication of the growing alcoholism problem in Micronesia (e.g., Mahoney 1974; USTTPI 1975), when in fact what they reveal is a remarkable continuity of drinking patterns through the years. For example, an American judge assigned to the Trust Territory court system in the 1950s "kept a running tally of the liquor cases" in Truk District and found "fully 50 percent of the criminal charges and convictions to be for drinking" (Toomin and

Figure 13. Among Truk's major imports are rice and beer

Media Class, Xavier High School, Truk

Toomin 1963:151). If anything, this statistic reveals a slight decline in arrests for drinking from that reported for a quarter of a century before, and it represents a sharp drop from the figure of 86 percent for 1937 (see above).

Another indirect measure often used to demonstrate that alcoholism and problem drinking are increasing in the Trust Territory in recent years is the monetary value of beverage alcohol imported into the islands (e.g., Nevin 1977:31; USTTPI 1975). For instance, Mahoney (1974:15) reports that in 1969 beverage alcohol accounted for 4.7 percent of all imports into the Trust Territory and that it was, in dollar value, the sixth largest single category of imported goods, exceeded only by building materials, machinery, rice, petroleum products, and clothing. This seems a startling fact until one discovers that it does not represent a departure from tradition at all. Alcoholic beverages made up 4.5 percent of all imports into German Micronesia (including Nauru) in 1912, and they constituted the seventh

43

largest single category of imports during that year (Prothero 1920). As in 1969, the import categories that exceeded beverage alcohol at this time were foodstuffs, building materials,[9] clothing, machinery, and fuel (in this case, coal).[10] Using government statistics, then, we see that relatively little has changed in Truk and Micronesia through the years as regards arrests for violation of the liquor laws and the place of alcoholic beverages among other imported commodities.

The Japanese offered important models of drunken comportment to Micronesians in the years between World Wars I and II. The annual reports to the League of Nations during the Japanese period give some idea of the amounts of beverage alcohol consumed yearly by those legally permitted to drink (see table 8). The per capita consumption figures in table 8 are probably a bit on the low side since many Japanese women either abstain or drink in greater moderation than their male companions (Japan 1933:33). But even discounting this possibility, the figures are rather staggering. For the seven years reported, the nonnative population over age 21 averaged 55.1 liters per capita per year, or approximately 14.5 gallons per year. By comparison, the leading state in the United States in per capita liquor sales during 1975—Nevada—had an adult per capita consumption of only about 11 gallons (*Des Moines Register* 1977). It is not clear whether the high consumption figures for Japanese Micronesia can be explained by the fact that the majority of the Japanese residents in the islands came from Okinawa, "which is recognized to be one of the wettest localities in Japan Proper" and where "women are not much behind men in the number of those addicted to drinking as well as in the quantity they consume" (Japan 1933:33).[11] What is clear is that a great deal of liquor

TABLE 8
Estimates of Beverage Alcohol Consumption in the Japanese Mandate by Nonnatives, 1928–1934

Year	Total estimated liters consumed in territory	Total nonnative population over 21 years of age	Number of liters consumed per capita
1928	552,830	8,539	65
1929	644,213	10,858	59
1930	631,261	12,566	50
1931	668,324	14,629	46
1932	879,569	17,636	49.9
1933	1,195,061	19,957	59.9
1934	1,376,666	24,451	56.3

Sources: Japan (1933:32, 1935:61, 1936:60).

was consumed annually by the expatriate population in Micronesia during the mandate period.

Given the heavy consumption of alcoholic beverages by Japanese nationals in Micronesia, it is useful to review briefly what is known of Japanese drinking customs and typical Japanese drunken comportment. Traditionally, alcohol addiction has not been a problem for the Japanese as it has been in so many European countries and in the United States. Yamamuro (1954) attributes this to the variety of religious influences that have helped shape modern Japanese culture: Confucianism (which encourages moderation but not abstinence from alcohol); Buddhism (which originally stressed abstinence in accordance with Buddha's fifth commandment); and Shintoism (which makes ritual use of sake in religious worship). Despite these religious teachings on total abstinence, alcoholism has become a problem in modern Japan (Yamamuro 1958).

According to Yamamuro, the Japanese have always been tolerant of and lenient toward misdemeanors by drunkards, viewing these lapses as "irresponsible and innocent." More recent work by Sargent (1967) indicates that this traditional attitude of permissiveness and protection of drunken persons continues to the present. Drinking was predominantly but not exclusively a male pursuit in Japan, and frequently the Japanese woman took on the role of ministering and caring for the drunken man (Sargent 1967). When women did drink, it was only rarely to the point of intoxication.

Japanese men are expected to "let their hair down" when drinking, and many of the strict rules of etiquette that govern sober social interaction are relaxed on such occasions. Men under the influence of liquor are not thought repulsive by their families or the general public, and "there is no rule which bids a man carry his liquor well" (Benedict 1967:285). Nearly all who have commented on Japanese drinking behavior specify that it is seldom accompanied by violence, quarreling, or aggression; on the contrary, it removes inhibitions to the display of affection. The highly controlled, stoic Japanese male is allowed to cry, sit in other men's laps, sing loudly, and generally make merry when drinking.

Japanese drinking occasions are a classic instance of what MacAndrew and Edgerton (1969) call "time out"—normal social rules are relaxed and "almost any foolish behavior under the influence of alcohol can be overlooked" (Sargent 1967:711). Along this same line, Dore asserts that "the etiquette of male drinking parties *requires drunkenness, and even, if the rice wine is not strong enough, a simulated display of drunkenness*" (1967:208; emphasis added). Finally, Nakane describes bars as places where Japanese men can "pour out all frustrations" to a sympathetic audience. She notes that "it is Japanese tradition that whatever is said in drink is excused and should be forgotten" (1970:125).

The picture that emerges from all this is one of fairly unrestrained,

45

jolly, nonviolent drunken comportment. Alcohol is treated as one of life's pleasures to be enjoyed primarily by men. Japanese drinkers are not held closely accountable for their words and acts when inebriated: drunken behavior is, first and foremost, *excusable* behavior.

As already indicated, by the Japanese period the Trukese had developed a violent style of drunken comportment based partially on European examples and partially on preexisting aspects of Trukese culture. The important notion the Japanese model of drinking provided Trukese was that of time out. While Micronesians already must have developed some sense of this from their earlier contacts with outsiders, the emphasis Japanese gave to drunken behavior as excusable behavior must have made a firm impression. Trukese men who traditionally had been encouraged to be aggressive against those outside their own kin-group or district were constrained by German and Japanese colonial laws against interpersonal aggression. While legally prohibited from drinking by the Japanese, the Trukese must have observed that the Japanese did not hold each other responsible for their drunken behavior. It took very little for Trukese to reach the logical conclusion that aggression when drunk would likely be excused by the Japanese authorities even though drinking *per se* would result in punishment.

Immediately after the U. S. Navy took control of the islands, procedures for repatriating Japanese military personnel were begun. Simultaneously, a host of new laws affecting Micronesians was put into effect. One of these laws was by this time familiar to the islanders. Contained in Proclamation No. 9, issued by Admiral Chester W. Nimitz, commander in chief of the Pacific Fleet, Article 5 of this law read: "The use, possession, sale, purchase, transportation, manufacture, gift or receipt of any intoxicating liquor is hereby prohibited except as authorized by my Military Government" (Richard 1957a:687). While events following the war presented a fundamental discontinuity for Micronesians, there was no lack of continuity in the official government stance on prohibition.

It is impossible to determine the effectiveness of Admiral Nimitz's proclamation as compared with the Japanese prohibition law, but it seems likely, given the awe in which Micronesians initially held the American military, that it was obeyed pretty well. As the shock of the war and its immediate aftermath wore off, however, Micronesians resumed their customary behavior of ignoring prohibition and trying to avoid detection when drinking. Many different Trukese informants have told me that it was American military men who first taught them the art of making home-brew from baker's yeast, sugar, and water.

Once the Japanese soldiers were repatriated and the machinery was set up for the Naval Trusteeship Administration (replacing the occupying forces), drinking in Micronesia returned to the state of affairs that had obtained before World War II. Reminiscent of the League of Nations requirement that the Japanese institute prohibition for natives in the mandated territory, the United Nations Trusteeship Agreement made it the obligation of the administering authority to control such traffic. The specific manner of control was left to the United States, however, and suggestions that absolute prohibition be enforced were opposed on grounds that

> the making of liquor from native sources, particularly the coconut palm, is so common and its use so obviously enjoyed by a large number of the natives and handled so moderately and unobjectionally by the vast majority that it is not deemed either practicable or advisable to attempt to stop such manufacture for individual, family or group use in accordance with established custom. [Deputy High Commissioner, Admiral Leon S. Fiske, quoted in Richard 1957b:484–485]

Although traditional, locally produced, alcoholic beverages were allowed, it was felt inappropriate for the civil administration to in any way encourage the sale or distribution of liquor to Micronesians from outside sources.

In February 1947, the Navy authorized the general sale of beer on Saipan on grounds that Saipan was a more acculturated area than the rest of the territory and that Saipanese were accustomed to beer. Soon thereafter, formal demands for imported beer were made by native leaders from both Palau and Truk, but these were ignored by the deputy high commissioner who recommended, on the basis of information he received from the civil administrators of each district, that no beer be imported into the Caroline and Marshall Islands.

A summary of the report from the civil administrator on Truk, contained in Richard (1957b:486–487), mistakenly claims that the use of palm wine had been universal there since aboriginal times and that beer and sake had been available during the Japanese period, presumably from bootleggers. More significant for our purposes, however, is the comment that

> the native palm wine was not very strong and the fermented form was not available in sufficient quantity to produce much drunkeness [sic]. When natives on Truk did succeed in getting beer, however, they became drunk on it: "A very few are moderate drinkers, stopping at a mild glow, more are happy drunks who sing sentimental songs until they lapse into blissful slumber, *but a large proportion tend to be fighting drunk, and the placing of beer on any free sale basis could be expected to cause a considerable amount of bloodshed.*" [Richard 1957b:486; emphasis added][12]

The fearsome Trukese drunk and the myth of Dread Hogoleu were alive and well in October 1948.

Throughout the Navy period, locally produced alcoholic beverages were permitted, subject only to local district or municipal regulation, but imported liquors were not legally available to Micronesians except for the sale of beer on Saipan. This state of affairs continued during the early years of governance by the Department of the Interior, in spite of the increasing clamor by Micronesians for the right to drink what they wished.

HAPPY DAYS ARE HERE AGAIN

Finally, in 1959, in response to the Palauans who had been the most vocal in the quest for freedom to drink beer during the Navy period and in years following, the high commissioner gave his blessing to a revenue resolution passed by the Palau District Legislature for the importation, public sale, and taxation of beer. Within a year, comparable bills had been introduced and passed in the remaining districts of the Trust Territory. These bills were amended beginning in mid-1960 to permit the sale and consumption of distilled spirits as well. In Truk District, the sale and consumption of beer became legal on June 1, 1959, subject to local option by each municipality (*Truk Review* 1959*a*:3).[13] Curiously, Truk was the last district in Micronesia to permit the legal consumption of beer (Toomin and Toomin 1963:151).

The Truk District Legislature set the beer tax initially at 10 cents per 32 ounces of beer, or 90 cents per case,[14] and the district administrator appointed a temporary Alcoholic Beverage Control Board to serve until the next session of the legislature. Beer sales were restricted to the evening hours during the week, and closing time was extended from 10:00 P.M. to midnight on Fridays. Sales were allowed from 9:00 A.M. until midnight on Saturdays and government holidays, and between noon and 10:00 P.M. on Sundays (*Truk Review* 1959*a*:3). Not long after beer sales were legalized, the fearsome Trukese drunk was once again out in the open. This is shown by a district law recommended by the Truk District Legislature later that year which prohibited "people from entering a beer hall with dangerous weapons such as knives, guns, fighting knuckles,[15] broken bottles or any objects used for fighting" (*Truk Review* 1959*b*:5).

The freedom to drink imported beer and liquors was gained at almost exactly the time that quantum leaps began to occur in U. S. funding for the Trust Territory. This funding led to the growth of government employment, improved schools, and a number of public works projects. These, along with a variety of other forces, precipitated the rapid growth of Micronesia's district centers through immigration. The district center on Moen Island in Truk, for example, grew at a rate of 8.3 percent per year from 1967 to 1973, by which time its residents accounted for 30 percent of the total Truk District population (Kay 1974:18).

With the growth of wage employment and population in the port towns has come a desire for leisure time entertainment and the where-withal to pay for it. As a consequence, bars and movie houses have sprung up to cater to the Micronesians' desire for an exciting night life. On Moen, in Truk, recreational businesses were limited to three poolhalls, three bars, and a single movie theater in 1965. A decade later, Moen boasted twenty-two poolhalls, six bars, nine movie theaters, and three bingo parlors (Akapito et al. 1975:2). Thus the appearance of an entertainment industry, including drinking establishments, is a recent phenomenon in Truk.[16] Of the six bars extant in 1975, four were opened in the early 1970s, one in 1966, and one dated back to 1959 (Akapito et al. 1975:7).

In 1976 there were still six bars on Moen, although the Truk Community Club, begun in 1959 when beer drinking first became legal, had folded and a new enterprise the "Happy Landings Bar" adjacent to the airport runway—had been added. In addition to these bars, which technically require demonstration of an official Truk District Drinking Permit before they will serve patrons,[17] package beer and liquor are available at five retail store outlets. The sale of alcohol is a most profitable business in Truk today. Mahoney (1974:table 3) estimates that the per capita purchases by members of Truk's "wet" municipalities jumped by 442 percent from 1969 through 1972. During the same period, the dollar value per capita of alcohol imports in Truk District rose from last place among the Trust Territory's six districts in 1969 to fifth place in 1970, fourth place in 1971, and first place in 1972 (Mahoney 1974:table 2). Clearly, the Trukese love affair with alcoholic beverages, begun less than a century ago and partially interrupted for nearly forty years, is now in full bloom.

A NEW DROUGHT HITS TRUK

Some months after this manuscript was completed, the Moen Municipal Council sponsored a referendum for registered voters of the Moen Municipality (who comprise, at most, one third of the total port town population) on the question of whether the sale and consumption of alcoholic beverages should continue or cease. The referendum was held in November 1977, and the overwhelming majority of those voting (reported to be mostly women and older men) voted for prohibition. The prohibition law that went into effect on January 15, 1978, has effectively halted all bar drinking.[18] The consumption of locally made alcoholic beverages by young men in and around the villages does not appear to have been much affected, however. Apparently the motive of the Moen Council in forcing the prohibition was mainly financial. Although the Truk District Legislature derived nearly one third of its total 1976–1977 budget from import duties and sales taxes on beverage alcohol, and the fees for local drinking permits, the Moen Council shared hardly at all in this bonanza. General expectations are that within a few months these financial differences will be resolved and Truk's newly imposed prohibition law will be lifted. It must be stressed that this new constraint has not stopped drunken fighting on Truk. If anything, it has made this pastime even riskier and hence more attractive than ever to its devotees (see chapter 3).

Pleading the Fifth

3

When a man lifts a cup, it is not only the kind of drink that is in it, the amount he is likely to take, and the circumstances under which he will do the drinking that are specified in advance for him, but also whether the contents of the cup will cheer or stupefy, whether they will induce affection or aggression, guilt or unalloyed pleasure. These and many other cultural definitions attach to the drink even before it touches the lips.

D. G. Mandelbaum,
"Alcohol and Culture"

FROM COCONUT TO RUM AND COKE

The single word *sakau* is used by Trukese to mean "alcoholic beverages of any sort" and "the state of drunkenness." This loan word from Ponapean, where it means kava,[1] occurs as both a noun and an adjective in Trukese. Thus one can say, "*A uun sakau*," 'He is drinking liquor', but one can also say, "*A sakau*," 'He is drunk'. Trukese subdivide the general category 'alcoholic beverages' into five major types: *pio* 'beer'; *uain* 'wine'; *wisiki* 'all distilled spirits'; *achi* 'fermented coconut toddy'; and *yiis* 'yeast or homebrew'. Sometimes the subclass *wisiki* is simply referred to as *meyi pwich* 'hot stuff', in reference to the burning sensation such beverages give when gulped straight from the bottle. Today's sophisticated port town drinkers identify *wisiki* by beverage type (e.g., gin, vodka, rum), and they also specify beer by brand name.

Among the five classes of alcoholic beverages recognized by Trukese, only fermented toddy and yeast are locally produced. Fermented toddy is made by cutting the growing spathe of a coconut palm and allowing the sap to drip into a container, usually a large *shoyu* bottle. The toddy—sweet and nourishing when first gathered and widely used as a baby food in the Carolines (see, e.g., Bates and Abbott 1958:76; Burrows and Spiro 1957:44)—is allowed to sit in an unwashed container until naturally occurring bacteria cause it to ferment, at which point it is drunk. Palms devoted to toddy production do not produce coconuts, and it was primarily this that motivated the German governor in Micronesia to ban toddy manufacture in the early part of this century. The home-brew known throughout Truk District as "yeast" is usually made in a large teapot or kettle by mixing a package of baker's yeast with sugar and water and allowing this combination to stand for about a day.[2] Because of its rather unpleasant taste, yeast is often flavored with instant coffee or the thick syrup from canned fruit before consumption. Compared to the array of alcoholic beverages that may be purchased on Moen today, fermented toddy, yeast, and the early trade alcohols only gave the Trukese a small taste of things to come.

In 1976, commercially produced alcoholic beverages from at least fourteen different countries could be bought from the package liquor outlets on Moen. Beers from the United States, Japan, the Netherlands, and the Philippines were available, as was a variety of still and sparkling wines from California and Portugal.[3] More than a dozen brands of bourbon, seventeen kinds of scotch, and fancy liqueurs from France, Denmark, and Mexico were on hand (table 9). Although priced higher than in the United States on account of steep transportation charges to Micronesia, a fifth of distilled spirits (excluding liqueurs) could be purchased for an average price of $5.35 a bottle. Cold beer was sold for about 50 cents a can from package outlets, although it commanded 75 cents a can in the bars. Wine—which is not a particularly popular item with Trukese drinkers—could be had for an average of just over $3.00 a bottle. Clearly, within a century, Truk had undergone a transition from coconut to rum and coke.

DRUNKENNESS AS TEMPORARY INSANITY

Like Admiralty Islanders, Trukese conceive drunkenness to be "both a state and a status" (Schwartz and Romanucci-Ross 1974:227). Imbibing alcohol produces certain more or less universal physiological effects (the state), but being drunk in public is also a social status, or, to use Goodenough's (1965) more specific terminology, a social identity. The social identity of the drunk in Trukese culture bears a striking resemblance to patterns of "crazy" behavior in several other cultural settings. It is not simply that contemporary drunkenness has become a functional equivalent of traditional warfare; rather, the introduction of alcoholic beverages

TABLE 9
Varieties of Distilled Alcoholic Beverages for Sale at Retail Outlets on Moen, Truk, April 1976

Beverage type	Number of brands available	Countries of manufacture	Average price per fifth
Vodka	10	Australia, Japan, U.S.A.	$4.67
Rum	10	Australia, Philippines, Puerto Rico, U.S.A., Virgin Islands	4.67
Tequila	3	Mexico	4.86
Blended whiskey	9	Canada, U.S.A.	5.15
Gin	4	U.S.A.	5.20
Other whiskey	2	Ireland, U.S.A.	5.59
Liqueurs[a]	17	Denmark, France, Mexico, U.S.A.	5.95
Bourbon	13	U.S.A.	6.04
Scotch	17	Scotland	6.56

Source: Author's field survey.

Note: All retail outlets selling package liquors on Moen were surveyed on April 19 and 20, 1976. These included Stop 'n Shop, Truk Cooperative, Truk Trading Company, and Tatasy & Sons Mart.

[a]The list of liqueurs is not exhaustive since I neglected to record those kinds available from TTC.

to Truk less than a century ago helped resolve one of the most fundamental difficulties in Trukese culture: how to allow for the legitimate expression of aggression. To become drunk in Truk is to put on a culturally sanctioned mask of temporary insanity. While insane/drunk one can express physical and verbal aggression that would bring strong disapprobation were one normal/sober.

Trukese believe that when one ingests an alcoholic beverage in whatever amount and of whatever sort, he is drunk and no longer entirely responsible for his words or deeds. Consumption of alcohol allows for an altered state of conscience in which one can get away with behaviors not normally permitted. In describing persons who are drunk, Trukese recurrently use several revealing words and phrases. Drunks are referred to as crazy, *meyi wumwes;*[4] they are likened to animals, *meyi wussun chëk maan;* and they cannot or will not hear or listen to others, *rese tongeni rongorong.* This notion of drunkenness as crazy, animallike behavior where the basic human capacity for reason is stripped away (one cannot reason with a drunk because he cannot hear) is fundamentally important for comprehending the Trukese attitude toward liquors and the behaviors of those who have consumed them. No matter how obnoxious and offensive a person's behavior when drunk, no matter what sort of mayhem a drunken berserker commits, he can always attempt to "plead the fifth" in order not to incriminate himself by pointing out that, after all, he was drunk, irresponsible, and did not know what he was doing.

Perhaps the nearest cultural analog to the identity of the Trukese drunk is the wild man behavior in New Guinea. Like Trukese drunks, New Guinea wild men are described by their fellows as crazy or insane (Clarke 1973:203, 208; Frankel 1976:114; Newman 1964:2), are likened to wild animals (Newman 1964:1) and are said to be deaf (Clarke 1973:199, 205; Frankel 1976:111). Also like Trukese drunks, New Guinea wild men are relieved of responsibility for their acts while deranged. Neither wild men nor their Trukese counterparts typically recall what happened during their episodes of derangement. Often such failure to remember episodes seems feigned, but it is a requisite part of both identities. Both New Guinea wild men and Trukese drunks frequently become violent, but such violence is never indiscriminate.[5] In New Guinea, young men are the ones most likely to become temporarily mad (Clarke 1973:199; Newman 1964:6–7),[6] just as in Truk it is young men who are the most likely to become drunk. Wild men and drunks feel no shame for their actions while "possessed." For the Trukese drunk as for the New Guinea wild man, the basic treatment is simply to let him act out his madness until he exhausts himself—after which, often with some sleep, his recovery is spontaneous. Both identities follow specific cultural patterns, that is, neither is a purely idiosyncratic way of acting. In both, too, the element of communication seems central—the wild man or drunk assumes the role of an actor to whom the remainder of the community plays audience. New Guinea wild men usually are presumed in local etiology to be possessed by ghosts or spirits of some sort. In nominally Christian Truk, where the missions have labored for a century to stamp out a belief in all ghosts but the Holy Ghost, drunks are simply possessed by alcoholic spirits. It is difficult to maintain that individuals affected in these ways are suffering from mental illness; far from being pathological, wild man behavior in New Guinea and drunken behavior in Truk are normal, acceptable social identities for resolving individual and interpersonal conflicts.

Equating drunkenness with insanity, craziness, or spirit possession is widespread in the cultures of Oceania and North America that lacked alcoholic beverages in the precontact period. For example, the Melanesians of Manus use terms glossed as 'crazy', 'dizzy', 'confused', and 'sick' to describe the inebriate state (Schwartz and Romanucci-Ross 1974:220). The New Zealand Maori word for being drunk, *haurangi*, "infers possession of the spirit by a primal deity" (Gluckman 1974:555). One of the more graphic metaphors for crazy drunken behavior comes from the Mortlock

Islands in Greater Trukese Society. Throughout this group of atolls, anyone demonstrating mental derangement or subnormality is called a "sardine," in reference to store-bought tinned fish, which come without heads. Those who become violent or disruptive drunks are also called "sardines" (Nason 1975). The Navajo concept of going crazy or being drunk involves "going wild," not knowing or caring what one is doing, and violent assaultive behavior (Kaplan and Johnson 1964). Reports for many other North American Indian groups echo this notion that drunks are literally out of their minds and hence not responsible for what they do (e.g., Berreman 1956 for the Aleut; Curley 1967 and Everett n.d. for the Apache; Hamer 1965 for the Potawatomi; Mohatt 1972 and Whittaker 1963 for the Sioux; Robbins 1973 for the Naskapi). Likewise, for those Amerindian tribes that had the dream quest, intoxication was included in the category of the supernatural:

> A person in the process of dreaming was considered somehow sacred; as was an intoxicated person. There must have been much similarity in the behaviour of the inebriated man and the dreamer half starved, full of expectations and hallucinating. Both could be seen running about seemingly possessed, disturbing the village with their screams. [Dailey 1968:50]

Clearly, then, a frequent means of explaining and classifying drunken behavior on the part of peoples who had not previously known it was to equate it with already known categories of behavior such as insanity or spirit possession, and this helps explain the Trukese view of drunkenness as temporary insanity. Comparing all Micronesians in the Trust Territory, Mahoney (1974:42) contends that "Trukese seem most convinced that once a person begins to drink he cannot hope to control himself, and as a consequence cannot be held rigidly accountable for his acts."

TRUKESE VALUES AND THE VALUE OF ALCOHOL

Every society has a set of core values and characterizations of the desirable that motivates and guides much of the behavior of its members. In every society, too, most individuals strive mightily to become and remain known as a "good person," and they work equally hard at avoiding becoming a "bad person." Greater Trukese Society is no exception to these statements.[7]

Basically, Trukese core values can be reduced to three pairs of polar opposites. When combined with each other, these pairs yield the Trukese conception of a good person and a bad person. Hence these basic values represent attributes of character. None of these attributes is an absolute; each pertains to acts or persons by matter of degree.

Following Caughey (1970), the fundamental constellation of values in Greater Trukese Society consists of:

Good person/desirable attributes	Bad person/undesirable attributes
Pwara 'bravery and power'	*Nissimwa* 'cowardice and weakness'
Mosonoson 'respectfulness and kindness'	*Namanam tekia* 'arrogance'
Ekiyek pwëcëkkün 'strong thought'	*Ekiyek pwoteete* 'weak thought'

Trukese seek to personify the attributes of a good person and avoid those of a bad person, and each individual's reputation for personal character is based primarily on performance.[8] The judgments of others derive from one's actions in what are considered to be relevant test situations.

The word *pwara* is used generally to refer to courage and power in all sorts of social situations, and in this sense it describes a person of competence. In its more limited sense, however, *pwara* denotes attitudes and acts associated with fighting and warfare and, in particular, an appetite for physical combat. *Bravery* refers not to a general unrestrained belligerence, but rather to a competent willingness to be aggressive in particular social contexts. According to Caughey,

> the classic test of *pwara* is a challenge to fight. The person of *pwara* shows no fear in such a situation, he acts ready, willing, and eager to fight to the death. He guides himself, it is said, by the following reckless disdain for self preservation, *määnö, ese määnö, nënnëë cëk* (lit. 'to die, not to die are the same to him'). It makes no difference whether or not the opponent is supported by henchmen or armed with some weapon, the man of "bravery" does not run. 'He does not show fear of people, of knives, of pain, or of death. He does not fear anything'. [1970:17]

Thus *pwara* in Truk closely resembles the concept of *machismo* in Central and Latin America, Spain, and some other Mediterranean countries. Both concepts embody the notion of defending one's personal reputation in public, even at the risk of death; both encourage the idea of never backing down from an older or stronger opponent; both partake of the idea that personal prestige can be enhanced by a demonstration of physical prowess. Neither concept emphasizes qualities of sportsmanship or chivalric elements; both stress a kind of manly superiority and competence partially demonstrated by dominating women in sexual conquests. These parallels between *pwara* and *machismo* are developed more extensively in chapter 5.

For contemporary Trukese males the classic test situation where public reputations are made and broken—a challenge to fight—arises most often following episodes of drinking. Bravery and physical prowess in combat, fearlessness and fearsomeness combined, are demonstrated to the public in acts of drunken violence. That this quest to prove oneself a man of bravery is nothing new in Truk is revealed by a significant statement in the early missionary literature. Describing mission life in Truk in the mid-1880s, at which time traditional warfare was still rife and alcohol had yet to be introduced, the Reverend Robert Logan wrote:

> There are many young fellows who seek the notoriety and popularity accorded to one who has killed some one. This is a cause of not a little of the fighting. There seems to be no shrinking from the guilt of murder. . . . [1887:252]

Among the several core Trukese values, *pwara* is paramount in the way it applies to drunken comportment. For this reason it is significant that Caughey finds *pwara* to always carry a strongly positive evaluation. When combined with respectfulness, bravery results in the ideal character type in Truk, known as *wesewesen pwara* 'true bravery'. Persons who possess this combination of traits are held in the greatest admiration.[9] In certain contexts, arrogance positively enhances bravery, and this combination of traits is called *mwääneson*. Persons who are *mwääneson* disdain the boundaries of normal human experience and are powerful and competent enough to break through them at will. Caughey suggests that many lineages and districts were willing to tolerate in their midst one or more individuals who were *mwääneson* to help protect their persons and interests from the aggressiveness of outsiders. Known as "the wall of the lineage or district," such men formerly led others in raiding and warfare; today it is they who deal most frequently with outsiders who try to make trouble. Such trouble often results from visits by young drunks from neighboring villages. On Moen, fights stemming from these visits assume the pattern I have labeled *weekend warfare*.

Next to bravery, the trait of *mosonoson* 'respectfulness' is held in highest esteem. A person known for bravery can be respectful with impunity because others fear him and will not recklessly challenge his reputation. One who is *mosonoson* is quiet and unassuming, kind and generous to others. The Trukese view such persons as holding themselves under control in normal situations although they may explode in destructive rage if crossed. Elements of admiration and awe are evident when people speak of the anger of a man of true bravery (Caughey 1970:25). By contrast, one who is *namanam tekia* is loud, assertive, crude, belligerent and given to bragging and ordering others about (Caughey 1970:21). Such a person's efforts to dominate and take advantage of others are despised in the extreme. Young men in the process of establishing personal reputations must walk a tightrope in how they express their toughness. To successfully negotiate the rope is to gain a desired reputation for *pwara;* to slip up is to fall into the despised category of one who is *namanam tekia.* Courage and assertiveness are an ideal only when tempered by respectfulness for others.

Strong thought and weak thought are tied rather closely to the traits discussed above. A person of strong thought tries not to be outdone in any activity or to lack anything that someone else possesses. Strong thought expresses the pervasive egalitarian current that runs through Trukese culture. By means of strong thought and its demonstration through acts of bravery and respectfulness, one proves oneself at least as good as others (and ideally, just slightly better). Thus one avoids "losing" to others, and one's personal reputation is further enhanced.

Strong thought and weak thought are identified with the sexes. *Ekiyek pwëcëkkün* also is known as *ekiyekin mwään,* or 'manly thought'. *Ekiyek pwoteete* has *ekiyekin feefin* 'womanly thought' as a synonym. A woman is praised if she demonstrates manly thought, but for her to show womanly thought is not cause for much comment. After all, "that's the way women are." For a man to fail to demonstrate manly thought, however, is personally and publicly shameful and opens him to gossip and derision. More than women, then, men must work at demonstrating their capacity for strong thought by performing up to standard in test situations.

Showing bravery, indicating strong thought, and being respectful together constitute the ideal set of personal attributes for Trukese. Particularly for men, these attributes must be established in the public mind through exhibitions of competence. Once established, they must be periodically revalidated by continued shows of competence. During his late teens and his twenties, the young Trukese male builds the personal reputation that will stay with him for the rest of his life. For a young man, this is a time of stress, a time of proving himself, a time of convincing others that he is indeed a man. Crucial to this period of life are those culturally established test situations in which public evaluations of competence are made. Many avenues for showing bravery and manly thought exist in Greater Trukese Society. Primary among these avenues today is the danger and risk associated with drinking spiritous liquors.

Nason (1975) has explained that the drinking behavior on Etal represents one part of a larger complex of masculine risk-taking. Among the risky endeavors engaged in by men, he lists gambling (especially blackjack), breaking municipal and church laws against alcohol use, "chug-a-lugging" liquor, the loud singing of World War II Japanese songs and Trukese love songs, traditional canoe voyaging, warfare, and the threat that a fellow drinker might become a sardine. Other elements must be added to this list, and certain of the risky endeavors Nason mentions require more extended comment.

58

Establishing a reputation as a competent man is a risky business in itself in Greater Trukese Society. Success is not assured, and its achievement must be continually sought. Fear of failure is high, and this is the source of no small amount of anxiety among young men. Traditionally, the perpetual raiding and fighting in Truk provided every young man with ample opportunity to display his true character. In a short but insightful piece entitled "Waging Baseball in Truk," Murdock holds that baseball, introduced by the Japanese, provided Trukese with an effective substitute for warfare.[10] He mentions preparations for baseball games in the late 1940s that followed almost exactly the traditional preparations for battle. Significantly, "women don't play because baseball, like war, is men's business" (Murdock 1948:292).[11]

Especially for outer islanders, where voyaging and navigation were of greater importance than in Truk Lagoon, taking part in open ocean canoe trips was a frequent means of proving oneself competent.[12] Men continue this tradition today in areas like the Mortlocks by setting out in small outboard motorboats from Truk proper to Nama and Losap or from Namoluk to Etal. These boats are much less seaworthy than the sailing canoes, and young men often undertake such voyages with limited fuel, a single motor, no oars or sails, and nothing aboard but liquid refreshment. In seeking an explanation for the low-key manner in which sailors in the Truk area approach the considerable risks associated with traditional canoe voyaging, Gladwin (1958) attributes their lack of concern to a lack of future orientation in Trukese personality. It is, however, more in keeping with other known features of Trukese life to attribute this willingness to risk the open sea in small craft to a desire to show bravery.

Several other risky or dangerous endeavors occupy young Trukese men. Severance (1976:144) notes that a way for exhibiting bravery on Piis-Losap is to spearfish in the deepwater passes and areas outside the reef where large sharks are common. A similar situation obtains on Namoluk where spearfishing provides young men with a productive means for showing bravery, strength, skill, and endurance. Young men and women are expected to engage in a variety of sweetheart relationships from their late teens to their early thirties (Goodenough 1949; Swartz 1958). Especially when one's lover is married, the sweetheart relationship involves considerable risk-taking (e.g., creeping into her house at night when she and her husband are asleep). Success in these extramarital affairs further demonstrates one's courage. Associated with the sweetheart complex is the practice of sending love letters via trusted intermediaries. In these letters young men express their undying affection and try to arrange assignations with their lover. But, as Swartz suggests (1958:479) the love letter itself is dangerous precisely because in writing and sending it a young man runs the risk of detection by his sweetheart's husband, with a fight or public confrontation sure to follow. Breaking the laws against drinking in "dry" municipalities like Etal or Namoluk entails a small element of risk, but other considerations such as local political competition may be just as important in explaining this behavior (Marshall 1975a; Nason 1975). But breaking the drinking laws on Moen involves a good deal more risk for those who are underage or do not possess a drinking permit.[13] Young men in Peniyesene flout these laws as a way of showing bravery; although the Moen Municipal Police make periodic forays through the village in search of illegal drinkers, young men usually escape easily by fleeing to the woods.

Another personal attribute that Trukese seek and admire is *tipetchem* 'learnedness or intelligence'. The major way of showing this valued trait today is to be successful in the formal educational system and subsequently to obtain a desirable government job based on one's acquired educational skills. To fail to be *tipetchem* is to be *tiperoch* 'unschooled or ignorant', a status that brings shame on oneself and one's family. Those young men and women who succeed educationally gain prestige and bolster their reputations as good persons in the process. Those who drop out, fail, or are thrown out of school erode their public images accordingly.

Every Trukese person has a reputation based on how well he or she embodies certain basic virtues that have been outlined above. Males more than females must actively prove themselves in establishing and maintaining their reputations for bravery and strong thought, although this should not be taken to mean that females do not have reputations to maintain. Males begin to build their public image during their late teens; this impression management becomes most intensive during their twenties. A variety of cultural avenues for taking risks and thereby demonstrating bravery exists, but primary among these avenues today is challenging and fighting others while drunk. Not only do individuals gain public reputations as good or bad, brave or cowardly, but lineages and districts also have such reputations (see Caughey 1970). The ways such reputations are made and defended are examined in chapter 4.

VENGEANCE AND VINDICATION

Given the active striving to build desirable public images on the part of so many persons, particularly young men, there are bound to be winners and losers in showdown situations. When a fight occurs, someone is usually bested by his opponent. When competition exists for possession of material goods that demonstrate one's manly thought, those who cannot purchase a new car, a motorboat, a Polaroid camera, or an expensive diving watch lose to those who can obtain these goods. When a member of one's lineage or district has been humiliated, beaten, or otherwise mistreated by outsiders, the score must be evened. Trukese hold grudges for a long time and await any opportunity to get even and tear down "the high and the mighty."

Much like the feuding between the Hatfields and the McCoys in American folklore, most interlineage and interdistrict warfare in aboriginal Truk consisted of a seesaw battle to remain one-up. When the other side took the advantage one could not rest until vengeance was had. This mentality, combined with a constant need to vindicate personal, lineage, and district reputations, remains strong in Truk today. A good person comes to the aid of his kinsmen, showing courage and manly thought as needs be. Traditionally and presently, one's rights are enforced mainly by the strength of support one can muster from one's relatives. Coming from a large lineage with a reputation for bravery makes it less likely that one will be trifled with by others. Hailing from a district known for its solidarity in the face of outside aggression gives one a distinct advantage when away from home since others will think twice before "playing with" one for fear of retribution. Even today, persons from different districts or islands in Greater Trukese Society often distrust those from other areas, although the extreme provincialism described by Swartz (1961:77) has begun to break down somewhat. In sum, a good person in Truk is one who seeks vengeance for wrongs done himself or his relatives. In obtaining this revenge one vindicates his own and his lineage's or district's reputation for strength vis-á-vis others. Revenge is a laudable motive in the Trukese scheme of things.

KUNG FU AND VODKA TOO

Many foreigners who have visited Truk within the past decade have commented on the great popularity of kung fu movies. Many no doubt would agree with Nevin's dour assessment that "the only things that seem to run well are the bars and the tatterdemalion movie theaters where, at the time of my visit, Kung Fu was in the ascendancy" (1977:143). There is no question that kung fu is in the ascendancy in Truk; my purpose here is to indicate why this is so by showing how kung fu intermeshes with Trukese values, the desire for vengeance, and the drunken comportment of young men.

We have noted above that young men develop reputations for manliness based in part on how they perform in physical fights with others. Any technique that allows a young man to gain an advantage over his opponents in these fights is highly sought after. Traditionally, Truk and other Carolinian Island societies had a system of special jujitsu-like holds and throws that was used in warfare. Knowledge of this system, called *pwääng* in Trukese, was carefully guarded and only passed on to others in one's network of close kin. As such, *pwääng* was and is viewed as a kind of esoteric lore, which also includes medicinal knowledge, navigational techniques, and information about genealogies and land tenure. Most young men in their late teens and early twenties do not know *pwääng* today; in some respects it is fair to view it as a dying art. Kung fu—another dramatic form of hand-to-hand combat—unlike *pwääng*, is available to all who have the price of admission to one of Moen's movie theaters.

While kung fu techniques observed in films are widely copied and practiced by youngsters on Truk, beginning with those only a few years old, the concern with strength and techniques of self-defense by Trukese young men runs deeper than this. Among those I know who have left Truk to attend college or vocational school outside the Trust Territory, virtually all have signed up to learn one or more of the martial arts like karate, judo, jujitsu, or tae kwan do. Armed with such specialized knowledge they return to Truk ready and willing to put knowledge into practice. Moreover, karate and jujitsu have recently been taught in limited private classes on Moen to those who can afford the price of lessons.

Trukese values stress never backing down from a fight no matter what the odds, and Trukese folklore often glorifies the underdog who overcomes all sorts of obstacles to reach his goal. As noted above, the notion of bravery does not involve sportsmanship; any way of defeating one's opponent in a fight is viewed as legitimate. All of this fits in perfectly with the "balletic violence" of kung fu movies. The apparently downtrodden and powerless hero eventually wins out in these films:

> In them one person, without technology, without money, without power, could confront the organisation, the protection racket king, and hit back. Perhaps they were simple fantasies of power, for they showed the character who, for decades, had just been one of the crowd in Western films taking control of his or her environment in no uncertain terms and in the most direct way possible. [Glaessner 1974:132]

Kung fu heroes are "little guys" who win. They show bravery and strong thought. But just as importantly, they show respectfulness as well. While the losers in kung fu movies are normally bigger and distinctly tougher looking than the winners, the winners triumph by adhering to "a ritual primarily involving a personal discipline tied to a generalized concept of justice and loyalty to the weak" (Glaessner 1974:22).

Beating an opponent in Truk may involve all sorts of "dirty fighting," but dirty fighting, in this sense, is an essential ingredient of the "ornate choreographies of violence" that have such a wide following in Truk: ". . . [these films] threw away the rule book and had absolutely no truck with avoiding taboo regions of the opponent's body; groin kicks and eye gouges were simply part of the repertoire" (Glaessner 1974:18). In kung fu and in Truk, too, no holds are barred.

62

Not only have the shrieks, blocks, kicks, and jabs of kung fu been copied by young Trukese, but some of the weaponry has been reproduced as well. Foremost among such weapons is the *nanchaku*, a two-sectional staff which, when whirled with skill, can reach a velocity of 150 mph along its perimeter. In Peniyesene and elsewhere, young men have made *nanchaku* from sections of steel pipe or from sawed-off legs of folding chairs, joined together with lengths of chain. These weapons are prominently displayed as young men loll about the village, and they are used when weekend warriors confront one another in drunken rumbles.

The continued success of kung fu films in Truk seems assured by the nature of their plots and by the desire of young men to copy fighting techniques seen on the screen. These films have been described as "elongated fight sequences" in which "the human weapon" has arrived, and they are said to have added "a new dimension to the iconography of violence" (Glaessner 1974). The thematic content of kung fu has struck another responsive chord in Truk with its emphasis on loyalty to kinsmen (especially loyalty to siblings) and on vengeance to wrongdoers. Glaessner (1974) describes these movies as "a series of revenge-motivated tournaments" in which "death to the enemy" is a frequent war cry.

While kung fu heroes often are decidedly ascetic, the young Trukese men who copy their exploits definitely are not. The lessons learned in movie theaters and practiced in shadowboxing with friends are put to effective use when drunk. In this context of "anything goes," the cry of *Waaaaaaaaa-ho*, known in Truk Lagoon as *akurang* and in the Mortlocks as *akapas*,[14] has become the war cry of the weekend warrior. Kung fu has left an indelible mark on Trukese drunken comportment.

BOONIES AND BARS

Drinking of alcoholic beverages on Moen occurs in two settings: in the bars and in the "boonies," as resident Americans call all areas of the island overgrown with brush. All bars but that at the Continental Hotel, which is seldom frequented by Trukese drinkers, are located downtown. Those who drink in the villages generally do so in the bush.

To a large degree the patrons of bars and the denizens of the boonies do not overlap. There are several reasons for this. Drinking in the bars requires quite a bit of money because the liquor served there is more expensive (it is sold only by the drink) and because of the Trukese custom of buying "rounds" for each other. On payday weekends, when the bars are filled to overflowing, some men spend their entire check buying drinks and return home with empty pockets. Technically, one must have a drinking permit to be served in the bars. Even though this requirement is enforced somewhat haphazardly, it serves to keep away most underage youths and those who have not purchased permits.

Many local bar patrons are men in their thirties and forties who make the rounds in a near-nightly ritual. Those few Trukese with serious drinking problems are usually to be found drinking in the bars. While fights may break out in the bars, Mahoney (1974:32) is correct in pointing out that get-togethers in bars are not always "sordid, drunken gatherings." On the contrary, there is music on the jukebox, a spirit of gaiety, jocularity, and good fellowship, and dancing and other amusements like gambling are available. It is also true, however, that these essentially all-male gatherings generate an exciting undercurrent of tension and

> once or twice an evening . . . there is a moment when one senses social electricity flashing: during the sudden silence that follows the entrance into the bar of men from a particular village or rival island faction; when nearby voices suddenly rise loudly in argument; or when a rock crashes upon the tin roof of the restaurant and everyone present jumps to his feet, prepared to do battle with someone, though with whom he is not quite sure. The scene, even to the music on the jukebox, is reminiscent of a Western movie. And, as with cowboy films, one feels certain that violence, accident or tragedy are not far away. [Mahoney 1974:32]

Most Trukese drinking still occurs in the boonies. A group of young men pool their resources to buy a bottle of whiskey and then let one among them, who has a drinking permit, buy the goods. The drinkers with their precious bottle return by taxi to the periphery of their home village where they sit in the bushes laughing, singing, swapping tales, and planning affairs with young women. The bottle is passed from one to the next and everyone present is urged to drink. These groups of "booze brothers" exert tremendous peer pressure on their members to drink and be drunk; it is a rare youth indeed who can refuse the blandishments of his peers (cf. Levy and Kunitz 1974:76; Mohatt 1972:271–272; Topper 1974:113).

No matter what his age, the Trukese drinker does not drink alone. The act of drinking is fundamentally a social act, and it loses meaning and pleasure if done without company. This is as true in the bars as it is in the boonies. The groups of young men who drink together usually consist of persons who are related (including *pwiipwi* 'created siblings'; see Marshall 1977). If the drinkers are not related, they are likely to come from the same village. Drinking is a dangerous activity and one wants his "brothers" around him for support. Of course, drinking also creates a context in which brother may turn on brother (see chapters 4 and 7), but this simply adds to the ambience of daring that surrounds this activity.

The general attitude among boonie drinkers is "the stronger the beverage the better." This attitude is less a matter of taste than of necessity. With several thirsty drinkers swigging from a single bottle, beer would not give "that desired feeling" as quickly, if at all. With stronger beverages, young men get what they feel to be the most for their money. Vodka and gin are relatively cheap per fifth when compared with other beverages (table 9), and the fact that they mix well with soft drinks adds to their popularity. Bar drinkers can afford to drink beer because they have the financial resources to drink can after can at 75 cents each; boonie drinkers cannot afford to be so casual with their much more limited resources.

THE LIFE CYCLE OF DRINKING

Drinking is almost exclusively a male activity throughout Greater Trukese Society, and it appears to have been so from first contact with alcoholic beverages.[15] Male and female informants alike are unanimous that drinking liquor by a woman is bad and wrong; those very few women who drink are viewed negatively and often are depicted as women of easy virtue. Some of the specific reasons for this are explored in depth in chapter 5 where alcohol use and sex roles are discussed. For the time being it will suffice to indicate the life cycle of drinking for males from childhood through old age.

Trukese males move through five life stages: *monukön* 'infant'; *ät* 'young male child'; *anuön* 'young man'; *mwään* 'mature adult male'; and *chienap* 'old person'. These stages are not bounded by rigid chronological markers. Rather, one moves from one stage to the next according to one's own pace of development. It is possible, however, to delimit each stage by rough age markers. Infants become young male children when they achieve a degree of mobility and independence from their mothers, usually around age 3 or 4 years. Boys remain as such until their mid-teens, at which time they become young men and begin to take on a variety of behaviors peculiar to persons in that category. As a male moves from his twenties into his early to mid-thirties, he imperceptibly slips from the young man category into that of a full-fledged adult man, an identity he occupies until physical decline and curtailed strength and activity cause him to be called an old person. Most men do not become old until at least age 60.

Under normal circumstances, alcoholic beverages are consumed only by young men or adult men. Until they are about age 18 or 19, most young men do not drink liquor or smoke tobacco more than occasionally.[16] A public sign that one is a young man and no longer a boy is to begin to smoke and drink. All young men in Peniyesene between the ages of 18 and 30 smoked cigarettes and nearly all of them drank liquor during the time of my field work.[17] Most of those who drank became intoxicated and assumed the social identity of the drunk in the community on numerous occasions. But on reaching their thirties, young men begin to change the style of their drunken comportment: their drunkenness becomes less flashy and less public, and they often switch from boonie drinkers to bar drinkers.

Consumption of alcoholic beverages is known throughout Greater Trukese Society as *angangan anuön* 'young men's work', and this tells us a good deal about the life cycle of drinking. Drinking and flamboyant drunken comportment are *expected* of young men; in Truk the young man who abstains is "abnormal," not the other way around.[18] Traditionally, young men have been viewed as high-spirited, irresponsible persons preoccupied with love affairs and image building. Young men are quite literally expected to engage in the proverbial "wine, women and song" in approximately that order. Their opinions are not sought on important lineage or community decisions. Until they become adult men, they do not begin to learn esoteric lore from their elders.

By the time they reach their mid-thirties nearly all males have altered their behavior from that appropriate to young men to that expected of mature adult males. Those who fail to accomplish this may be taunted with the question, Why are you doing young men's work? During their tumultuous twenties, men build their reputations for manly thought and strength. By the time they become adult men, their character is largely fixed in the public eye. Even though many adult men continue to drink, in some cases very heavily, what is important for our purposes is that their behavior after consuming liquor is radically different from that of young men. Specifically, the fighting, swaggering, kung fu, and ear-splitting war cries get left behind. As men move into their late forties and fifties they take on ever greater responsibilities in their communities. Many become leaders in the church, a major requirement of which is to eschew liquor. Factors such as this, coupled with their own feelings of declining physical strength, lead most men to give up alcohol entirely from about age 50 on except on very rare occasions.[19]

The dramatic public display of drunkenness serves as a behavioral marker demarcating *anuön* 'young man' as a life stage for Trukese males. A sign that one has come of age is to begin the swaggering, staggering, boisterous drunken behaviors that lead to situations in which bravery and strong thought are tested. Abandoning this arresting style of drunken comportment and taking on the quieter, though not necessarily more sober, behaviors of an adult man just as surely mark one's movement out of the young man category. Our primary focus in the remainder of this book is on the drunken style of young men—the style of the "fearsome Trukese drunk." In seeking to understand this behavior we first need some descriptive facts to work with.

Drunkenness in Peniyesene: Case Studies

4

Drunkenness is widely accepted in Micronesia as an excuse for otherwise unacceptable behavior, and young men pass abruptly from quiet drinkers to belligerent drunks. After a night of drinking, after other people have gone to bed fights of startling violence break out and rage through the hot, dark streets. Often they begin with fists and move on to weapons. More and more frequently they end in serious injury or death.

D. Nevin, The American Touch in Micronesia

ALCOHOL USE IN PENIYESENE: AN OVERVIEW

It is now appropriate to turn to some concrete examples of the temporary insanity, tests of bravery, and occasional game of death that make up weekend warfare in Truk. Before doing so, however, some general comments on drinking and drunkenness in Peniyesene are in order.

In March 1976 there were fifty-seven males in the Peniyesene resident population between the ages of 18 and 35; of these, fifty were known to consume alcohol during the research period. Eight other males in the resident population over age 35 were also known to drink during this time.[1] In understanding alcohol use in the village it is helpful to examine the cases of those young men who did not imbibe.

One nondrinker had just turned 18 and was still in high school; he could reasonably be expected to start drinking within a year or two. Another nondrinker, age 20, came from the Faaychuk area of Truk and was living temporarily in Peniyesene with a created brother; it is entirely possible that he drank quietly and that this escaped my notice. A third individual, age 21, had had his father killed in a drunken brawl (see Case 11 below) and was largely responsible for supporting a sizable extended family on his small income. This responsibility, coupled with his mother's continued urgings to forswear alcohol lest he follow in his father's path, appeared sufficient to keep him from the bottle.[2] A fourth nondrinker, age 25, was mentally retarded, of childlike behavior, and remained secluded with his family all the time. The fifth nondrinker, a young man of 28 years, was the head of the Catholic-sponsored *mwichen asor* service program in Peniyesene. He seems to have been profoundly influenced in his attitudes toward alcohol during his education at the Ponape Agricultural and Technical School (PATS), run by the Jesuit fathers.[3] Two other nondrinkers were both age 34 and had been wild drunks a few years before. Both were employed in responsible government jobs and were clearly in the process of altering their former 'young man' behavior to bring it into accord with their new identities as adult men. We see, then, that special circumstances surround every case where a Peniyesene young man did not drink.

The oldest consistent drinker in the village was 47 years old, and only one other man in his forties drank liquor on a regular basis. Both of these men imbibed only in the bars, drank almost every day, and appeared dependent on ethanol. Inquiries in the village as to who were heavy drinkers inevitably elicited the names of these two men along with comments on the unusualness or inappropriateness of their behavior given their age and station in life. Both men were employed full-time in the wage economy, both were married and had fathered numerous children. The families of both suffered somewhat as a consequence of the substantial sums these men spent on booze. In comportment each was a quiet, "happy" drunk who came home and went to bed following an evening binge. At least one of them frequently missed work while recuperating from the previous night's festivities.

Only one other person in Peniyesene drank frequently enough and in sufficient quantity to be labeled an "alcoholic" using Jellinek's formula for "gamma alcoholism" (Jellinek 1960).[4] This man, in his late thirties, was employed full-time but spent many of his waking hours tippling in the downtown bars. Rowdy, obnoxious, and verbally belligerent when drunk, he nevertheless was not involved in any fights in the village during the research period.

Actual inebriation by one or more Peniyesene males was observed on an average of three to four days a week throughout the field-work pe-

Figure 14. The village "battleground" in Peniyesene, with the local poolhall-cafe (left) and the author's house (center)

riod. Since my research involved a number of other topics, some of which took me out of the village for most of the day once or twice a week, it is likely that the incidence of drunkenness was even higher than this. Moreover, this figure does not take into account the drunken men from other villages who regularly ventured into Peniyesene, particularly men from Peniya and Tunnuuk. The number of drunks reeling about usually peaked on weekends, although drunks might be encountered at any time of the day or night throughout the week. Sundays proved a particularly "sodden" day, so much so, in fact, that we began calling Sunday *ranin fiyu* 'day of fighting' instead of by its Trukese name of *ranin fäl* 'day of church'. Payday weekends every two weeks led to binge drinking by much of the village's young male population.

Between Tunnuuk and Peniyesene at the sharp bend in the road by Wupweyin (map 5), and beneath a huge banyan tree along the road between Peniya and Söpwüük are areas where young men often congregate to drink and fight with warriors from adjacent villages. Peniyesene and Peniya, however, blend together at the head of the bay in a continuous line of houses, leaving no place in between in which to congregate. Consequently, the main road near where the villages join by the bridge and the Peniyesene poolhall serves as a battleground for young warriors from these two districts out to prove their bravery (figure 14). As it happened,

69

my family and I lived in a house at the junction of Peniyesene's two main roads directly opposite this battlefield, and thus we commanded a sweeping view of all that took place there.

On a "good" weekend, drunks would swagger up and down the road in the vicinity of the poolhall or wander along the road leading up the valley glowering at passersby and looking for others to fight. At least one or two fights would break out on the battleground between males of different Peniyesene lineages or between young men from different villages. During the day challenges would be shouted back and forth between Peniya and Peniyesene, and the warm nights would be rent with war cries as drunks paraded through the village spoiling for a fight. When violence broke out during daylight hours, a large audience quickly formed, though women and children usually were careful to keep a discreet distance. Once or twice a weekend at most, a Toyota pickup loaded with a half dozen husky armed policemen would cruise through the village looking for illegal drinkers and disturbers of the peace. When the police drove back toward town, the drunks would reappear from hiding and the weekend warfare would continue as before. Let us turn now to some specific case descriptions of drunkenness in Peniyesene taken from my field notes.

CASE 1: THE CASE OF THE BROKEN LOUVRES

X was thrown out of high school in his senior year for repeated violation of the rule against drinking by students.[5] Age 24, unemployed, married, and the father of a small child, he lived in Peniyesene with his parents, on whom he was dependent for life's essentials. X's father had a good job and regularly gave him money, which he used to go drinking with his cronies. On the day in question, however, X had asked for money and had been refused.

After drinking downtown on the dock with some friends for a while, X found another young man from Peniyesene with a bottle of whiskey and retired to the brush near his home with his "booze brother." After a time X emerged from the bushes, strode to the village battleground, and began whooping and aiming kung fu kicks at passing taxis. On seeing this, the husband of a senior woman in X's lineage, accompanied by X's drinking partner, dragged him protesting into his parents' house. No one was at home at the time and before long trouble began.

X started pounding heavily on the thin walls of his parents' dwelling before racing outside where he groveled for rocks to throw at the house. All the while his senior kinsman spoke soothingly to him. After X had flung a few rocks at the house, he allowed himself to be led away to a nearby cookhouse. Before long, he wove back into view, staggered in an exaggerated fashion for a while in front of the audience that had begun to gather and then suddenly ran in a straight line to a nearby house from which he shortly emerged clutching a *nanchaku*. Striding purposefully now, he headed back to the battleground, rushed at a young woman and a younger boy (who simply grinned and walked away a little faster), and then disappeared into the poolhall.

Within a few minutes, his grandfather, a well-preserved man in his late sixties, pulled him out of the poolhall and alternately pushed, dragged, and wrestled him back toward his parents' house. X resisted but did not actually fight his grandfather. Harsh words were exchanged, there was a great deal of commotion as X emitted piercing "war cries," but no blows were struck. Eventually, the grandfather got X home and into the dwelling with the door closed.

Almost immediately X smashed down the front door with a series of kung fu kicks and then began swinging his *nanchaku* wildly about the house. During the melee that followed, in which his grandfather loudly berated him, X shattered the glass louvres in the main window of the house, cutting his hand in the process. The destruction inside the house continued for approximately ten minutes, by which time a crowd of forty or fifty persons had gathered to watch. After a while, the grandfather was able to grab the *nanchaku* and throw it through the remains of the door where one of X's sisters scooped it up and ran off with it. At this, X again ran out of the house and picked up rocks which he began throwing at his grandfather's house, the family cookhouse, his parents' house, and at the bystanders who were enjoying his antics from a prudent distance. All the while, X whooped, staggered, and shouted his anger to all listeners.

An hour later, X knocked on our door and I let him in. He slumped down on our couch, panting and whimpering a bit. I asked if he wished to drink coffee or smoke a cigarette, but he declined in favor of a glass of cold water. Bringing his water, I sat down next to him to chat. He told me everyone in Peniyesene was afraid of him and it was well known that he could strike people. He said, unsolicited, that he had shown them his bravery. When I asked why he was angry with his family, he responded, "Because they don't listen or pay attention to me." At this moment, he pointed out the gash on his thumb incurred when he smashed out the louvres, and I offered to clean and bandage it, for which he seemed grateful. As I worked on his wound, we continued our conversation with X speaking in English much of the time even though our normal interactions were in Trukese. He asked me questions about Bruce Lee, Elvis Presley, the Beatles, and kung fu and volunteered that he could not obtain a job because he had not completed high school. When I suggested he might enroll in the adult education high school equivalency program or seek vocational training, he sneered and said that what matters in Truk is not what you know but who you know if you wish to work. At one point in our talk he abruptly stated, "I'm not drunk," and said that he would not cause any trouble at my house. This statement had been underscored earlier by his studious avoidance of our house as a target when flinging rocks in every other direction. After about twenty minutes, X left our house and walked swiftly in a straight line up the valley road to bathe in the river.

CASE 2: THE CASE OF THE BROKEN SKULL

The trauma sustained in a drunken brawl put Y at death's door, has permanently affected his behavior, and led to an outbreak of hostility between Peniyesene's two largest lineages that continues to influence drunken brawling in the village to this day.

Several years ago a sizable group of young men was drinking together in the woods near the village. As frequently happens in such dangerous situations, an altercation developed and the booze brothers split into two groups of fighters according to their primary kinship loyalties. In the brawl that followed, members of one group produced a can of Mace, which they sprayed in the faces of several of their opponents, rendering them helpless. Thus incapacitated, Y was struck on the top of the head with a large rock. The blow split his skull, knocked him into a coma, and resulted in permanent brain damage. He was rushed to the hospital and subsequently evacuated by air to Guam, where he underwent extensive neurosurgery. Today, at age 25, he has somewhat recovered although he has never returned to his former self. According to members of his family, he cannot abide large groups of people or lots of noise. Consequently he lives with relatives up the valley somewhat removed from the daily hubbub of village life. Although his doctors warned him not to drink again, he does so rather frequently. When Y appears in a drunken state, everyone scatters, and people are genuinely afraid of what he might do while inebriated.

Coincident with Y's medical evacuation to Guam, open warfare broke out in Peniyesene between members of the two lineages involved in the initial brawl. Vengeance was clearly called for, and "Death to the enemy" was the cry. Rifles, knives, machetes, and other weapons were mobilized, and only swift action by the Moen Municipal Police and subsequent discussions between the leaders of the two lineages averted further bloodshed. But, as noted in chapter 3, Trukese hold grudges for a long time. An analysis of the intravillage fights during the period of my research reveals that about one quarter were between members of these two lineages; the injury to Y several years back is frequently cited as an explanation for this.

CASE 3: THE NAPOLEON COMPLEX

Although many Trukese men are big, and nearly all are husky and well built, "Napoleon" was none of these. Slight of build, short of stature, and young in years (age 20), he, perhaps more than others, had to work to prove his manhood. In trying to do so, however, he usually ended up merely reinforcing the public view that he was of little consequence or promise.

It was a Sunday afternoon and Napoleon had been swigging gin with several others on the periphery of the village. I encountered him weeping openly while his father's sister upbraided him in front of several women and children for drinking. In the midst of this scolding, Napoleon got up and walked about twenty yards to where a group of sober men was seated beneath some coconut palms. Approaching the group, Napoleon singled out the only adult man among them, a man of rather corpulent build in his late forties, who was married into Peniyesene from a distant district and was therefore largely without local lineage supporters. Unprovoked, Napoleon walked up to this man and struck him in the chest. Surprised but not stunned, the man did not fight back and one of the young men in the group who was related to Napoleon tried to get Napoleon to leave. The latter's response was to erupt with blows, hitting and kicking at his kinsman until a well-aimed kung fu shot to the face knocked him backwards into a coconut palm. Fed up with this brazen attack, another young man in the group—a clan brother of the one just struck—grappled ever so briefly with Napoleon, lifted him bodily in the air, and flung him hard to the ground where he lay moaning with the wind knocked out of him.

Napoleon's drinking companions hurried over at this point, helped him to his feet, and led him away as he screamed imprecations at those he had attacked. Shrugging off his companions and shrieking all the while, he ripped his shirt in half and threw it to the ground, shouting that he was going for a knife with which to kill the one who had just beaten him. As he ran toward his house to get his weapon, the women who had been watching told the group of men who had been attacked to leave, which they did. Napoleon's mother and sisters hide all knives and machetes whenever he drinks in anticipation of situations like the one that had just unfolded. After rummaging through his house, Napoleon had to content himself with a fishing spear which he brandished wildly on his return to the scene a few minutes later. Following some more shouting and prancing about, a lineage brother took the spear away from him and led him homeward.

Later that day, Napoleon continued his antisocial outbursts. Angry at his sister for hiding his knife, he attempted to hit her first with a rock and then with a bottle, both of which she dodged. The second fist-sized rock he hurled, however, struck her hard in the back and she collapsed wailing on the spot until led away by other young women. Although several senior relatives were present and observed these proceedings, no effort was made to discipline Napoleon in any way.

As Napoleon wandered about the village looking for trouble, he encountered another drunk with whom he fought. Though bested in this fight too, he managed to land one or two good kung fu blows on his opponent. This angered the opponent's sister, who stood by watching the struggle. Out of loyalty to her sibling, she immediately set off in search of Napoleon's sister. On finding her, she instigated a great hair-pulling, ear-splitting, dress-ripping fight, which took a half dozen people to break up. Thus poor Napoleon's sister was beset from all sides as a result of her brother's drunkenness.

CASE 4: BEATING UP BROTHER

The case of Z demonstrates how the most serious and forbidden aggression against close kinsmen may rise to the surface when Trukese are under the influence of alcohol.

Z was a strapping lad of 22. He left school after the eighth grade to assist his recently divorced mother in providing for his many younger siblings. He was one of the few young men in Peniyesene who regularly worked on the land growing taro and preparing copra for sale at the TTC. Z was an extremely pleasant young man who did not drink often. When he did drink, he usually became what Trukese call a *mosonoson* drunk— one who is quiet, happy, perhaps a bit giddy, and fun to be around.

On the day in question, however, Z was anything but *mosonoson*. Angry at his older lineage brother, Z got drunk in order to spew out his rage. Confronting his brother at the family homesite, he struck at him, and others immediately intervened. His maternal grandmother stood over him at the side of the road where he collapsed and loudly screamed out her anguish and disappointment at him. Z thrashed about in the road, yelling that he had no relatives in Peniyesene. He was finally led off by a distant patrilateral female kinsman who took him to her house to "cool off."

Instead of cooling, Z's anger grew and welled up within him. Still drunk, he returned to his brother's house, this time to be confronted by his intended victim's sister with whom he began exchanging heated words. Enraged at his arrogant behavior, this woman's husband (age 28) grabbed a fishing spear and grappled with Z. In the ensuing fracas Z was stabbed just below the eye and was rushed to the hospital for treatment. Luckily, the spear did not hit his eye, and a few stitches and a tetanus shot repaired the physical damage. The social damage done would take a little longer to heal.

CASE 5: I SAW IT AT THE MOVIES

A and B were *pwiipwi winisam*—brothers by virtue of both being descended from males in a single lineage. Although B lived in Tunnuuk a mile or two away, the two young men (aged 19 and 23, respectively) often got together to drink. On this particular day they had a fifth of vodka, now half empty, and they were making their way through the village en route up the valley. When they reached the battleground, however, B felt compelled to demonstrate his bravery to the people congregated near the poolhall.

B began alternatively bellowing like a bull and issuing the standard Trukese war cry while accosting passing taxis by standing squarely in the middle of the road. Once he had halted a vehicle full of people, he went into a shadowboxing routine employing leaps, pirouettes, and stiff poses in the fashion of Bruce Lee. A, and C—who was sober—sought to drag B away from the battleground, but to no avail. The antics continued for some minutes providing a spectacle for a growing audience of children who had been attracted by the din. Finally, A handed the half-full bottle of vodka and his towel to a young kinsman of 12 to hold while he tussled with B in a renewed effort to get him moving up the valley. By this time, B had warmed to his role and resented A's interference. The tussle turned into a wrestling match, which concluded with A and B wallowing and rolling in a large mud puddle to the delight of the gathered children. Finally, an older man related to both young men succeeded in herding B up the valley while A—vodka again in hand—trudged along behind.

CASE 6: PLAYING CAT AND MOUSE

It was about 5:00 P.M. at midweek. Commuters were returning to Peniyesene and the villages farther out, as taxi after taxi careened past with its overload of passengers. Suddenly, a familiar Peniyesene vehicle raced up to the main intersection, quickly dropped off two village young men and hurried on up the valley road with two others in the front seat. No sooner had they disappeared from sight than a rickety old pick-up from Söpwüük roared up at an excessive speed and swerved into the parking area by the poolhall. The two young warriors in this truck sat racing their motor, swilling Schlitz beer, and giving threatening looks to everyone around. The sober young men from Peniyesene with whom I was sitting in my front yard acted scared.

Meanwhile, the vehicle from Peniyesene had turned around up the valley and its driver now edged cautiously back down the valley road to see if the coast was clear. As he approached where we were sitting, my companions warned him that his pursuers were still about, whereupon he quickly backed up, turned around, and hurried off in the opposite direction. Some minutes later, he (age 28) and his companion (age 34) again appeared and this time, just as they reached the intersection, the Söpwüük warriors careened out of the poolhall lot and raced up next to the Peniyesene vehicle, nearly crashing into it in the process. They sat there glowering disdainfully at their quarry while the local warriors failed to meet their gaze. Smirking over their triumph in this war of nerves, the Söpwüük toughs slowly backed out, conspicuously discarded their empty beer cans on the village battleground, and drove leisurely off in the direction of home.

CASE 7: HELP! POLICE!

Young men in Truk have little respect for the Moen Municipal Police, and they often attack policemen with knives and other weapons. It is for this reason that policemen on patrol for drunks always travel in groups of from four to six. Part of the reason young men do not respect the police is revealed in the case that follows.

D was from Mecchitiw village near downtown, though his father was from Peniyesene. In build he resembled a typical Polynesian more than a Micronesian, standing about 6 feet 3 inches and easily weighing 225 pounds. His imposing size and his reputation as a tough cop made him a young man of considerable renown whom few wished to cross. Despite his widespread reputation for bravery, D periodically felt the need to reaffirm his standing.

My first inkling that something was up came on hearing women scream right outside my house. Poking my head out the front door I was just in time to see a woman of 50 run by yelling in terror and pursued by D (out of uniform), who at that very moment stooped to grab a fallen coconut to throw at his victim. Simultaneously, other women, obviously frightened, were screaming and shouting and running in all directions while several small children began crying. As D hurled the coconut, missing his intended target, a sober young man related to him patrilaterally quietly suggested that he cease and desist. This "provocation" led D to turn on his much smaller relative who offered little resistance. Then D saw me watching him from a few feet away. His demeanor changed instantly, and he let go of his latest victim. In an apologetic tone he began trying to explain his actions to me in English. I asked if he wanted a drink of water, hoping to divert his attention from those he was threatening, and he said, "Yes." As I was getting his water his three drinking companions from Mecchitiw drove up and tried unsuccessfully to get him into their car. As I brought his water, he took off after a woman bystander, shouting, *"Met? Met?"* ('What do you want?') in a nasty tone. The woman scurried into her house, and D picked up a large rock and headed for the poolhall, scattering people (including young men) before him as he went. After some shouting inside the poolhall, his companions were able to corral him, force him into their car, and drive off with him toward town.

76

CASE 8: BRAVERY ABOVE ALL ELSE

Scars are worn with pride by Trukese men and they may be inflicted purposefully as well as accidentally in fights (see chapter 5). However obtained, scars are a visible sign of courage. For example, Gladwin and Sarason (1953:111–112) mention traditional Trukese warriors employing the tactic of cutting their arms in front of opponents to intimidate them with their unflinching bravery before a fight. E has a large scar on his arm of which he is exceedingly proud.

Drinking far up the valley one day about three years ago with F and G, E discovered that his companions planned to fight each other, and he left. On returning sometime later, he found F and G having at it, but G had a large knife, and F was unarmed. Hoping to prevent a murder or serious injury, E, who was about 23 at the time, stepped in in an attempt to remove the knife and make the odds more equal. On his third effort to take the knife away from G, E was slashed deeply along his arm near the elbow. Bleeding profusely from venous wounds, he was taken to the hospital to be sewn up. On learning that the doctors would insist on reporting the incident to the police, however, E left the hospital without being treated for fear he would be jailed for having no drinking permit. Others viewed this stoicism with admiration as an act of daring and bravery.

CASE 9: SOME DAYS IN THE LIFE OF A TYPICAL WEEKEND WARRIOR

M was 25 years old, of medium build, married, without children, and gainfully employed in a government job. He had received vocational training abroad and may be said to have "made it" in the present system on Truk. He was also an incorrigible drinker. What follows is an account of some of the drunken disturbances in which M was involved over the period of my research. M's case is fairly typical of many other "weekend warriors" in contemporary Truk.

Sunday, February 1, 1976. M and his 21-year-old brother, also employed, were drinking and got into a wild fisticuffs and kung fu match on the village battleground at about 3:00 P.M. They were finally pulled apart by adult male and female relatives, who took them off to different houses. The next day I heard three young women discuss this fight with excitement and admiration.

Saturday, February 14, 1976. Along with four other young men, M dashed down several shots of straight whiskey in an area not far removed from my house late in the afternoon. A woman of 70, the grandmother of one of the drinkers, happened by and, to my great amazement, took a swig from the bottle.[6] The drinking group was in a good humor, and one drunk made his lineage sister hold his hand. M's mother-in-law hid in her house because, as she stated later, she was afraid of him. The drinkers sang along with the radio and played affectionately with a toddler and an infant being held by the young women present (who did not drink). Eventually, this scene of domestic tranquillity was broken up by impending darkness.

Saturday, March 13, 1976. M was "high" and approached me speaking his best American slang ("Hey man, how's things?"). We chatted amiably for awhile—with M speaking English exclusively and me responding in Trukese—during which time he repeatedly called to my son by name. M then wandered off toward the poolhall and half an hour later I saw him being led home by a sister.

Sunday, April 25, 1976. M and a workmate from Söpwüük village were drinking a fifth of Barclay's vodka at about 3:00 P.M. When I encountered them their bottle was nearly empty. At about 6:30 P.M. a fight broke out on the village battlefield, and I ran to see. M and a young warrior from Peniya were rolling around in the dirt slugging at each other until pulled apart by several other young men. As they were dragged off in opposite directions the combatants hurled repeated taunts and threats at each other (e.g., "Remember this, young men of Peniyesene," and "Your father!"). Just after 8:00 P.M. I discovered M's wife hiding in the shadows behind my house. When I asked if she was all right, she said, "Yes," but that she had run out of her house because her husband had come home drunk and she disliked his drinking.

Monday, May 10, 1976. M stayed home from work to get over the effects of three straight nights of drinking on a payday weekend.

Sunday, June 20, 1976. During an extended interview with M concerning Trukese drinking and his own drinking history, he mentioned that he had had a drinking permit until recently when his wife tore it up because she did not want him to drink so much.

CASE 10: INEBRIATION, REJECTION, AND RETALIATION

Suicide is today the leading cause of death among Micronesians age 15 to 30. Hezel (1976) observes that these deaths follow a quite regular pattern all over the Trust Territory. Most victims are young males from districts in eastern Micronesia (especially Truk and the Marshalls) who have just had an emotional argument with a close relative or friend. Most had been drinking alcoholic beverages before committing suicide, which is usually done by hanging.

By virtue of suffering over one half of all suicides in the Trust Territory from 1975 to 1976, Truk District has "acquired the unenviable title of the suicide capital of Micronesia" (Hezel 1976:9). Hezel argues that neither the drinking nor the family quarrel that normally precedes these suicides can explain them. Rather he suggests that we view them as acts of vengeance "against those who are the objects of the victim's anger." In

Greater Trukese Society, at least, consumption of alcohol bolsters the young man's courage to do deeds of bravery (including killing himself), but suicide itself is an act of aggression against close kinsmen who have somehow pushed the victim over the brink of despair by rejecting him in an emotional confrontation. Under such circumstances, his only way for vengeance is to kill himself and let his tormentors suffer guilt thereafter. The case described below illustrates this.[7]

Q first came into my view out on the battleground as his older brother held him firmly by his long, shoulder-length hair and pushed him roughly ahead. Suddenly, Q broke and ran past my house back toward the poolhall yelling like crazy at everyone in general. A few moments later, Q dashed back up the valley road, still screaming shrilly, and burst into a homesite as if to cause trouble there. The next thing I knew, someone grabbed Q and threw him hard into the sloppy mud puddles in the valley road. To my astonishment the man who had forcibly reprimanded Q was none other than his father, a man in his early fifties. The father sat on top of Q and easily got the upper hand as they continued to grapple. A sober young man from the household Q had threatened to attack watched them but made no attempt to intervene.

The wrestling and shouting continued for several minutes until Q's father lost his patience and began violently beating his son in the face and chest. When his father finally released him, Q leapt up instantly and charged wildly down the valley road toward my house, wailing eerily. Two young women in their early twenties, one of whom was holding a small child, were standing in the road. Q rushed straight at them but they did not move. On reaching them, Q leapt up and slapped one loudly on the back with his open hand and then fell in a heap on the ground beside them. He lay there a moment, got up, and ran off toward the poolhall once more. Within minutes his older brother and father had collared him and again began dragging him up the valley road against his will. As before, he began struggling violently with his father until once again his father threw him down and jumped on him, this time choking him briefly. Q's father then stood up and strode off, leaving him lying very still in the road, watched over by his brother. Following a five-minute interlude in these fast-breaking events while he just lay in the road, Q got up slowly, and his brother led him homeward.

I learned that Q, age 22, had been drinking with some other young men and was found by his father. His father had earlier forbidden him to drink and had sought unsuccessfully to get all his sons to take the *mwichen asor* pledge; seeing Q drunk so angered him that he lost his temper and the result was what I observed.

The next day I learned that Q had gone home and flung himself headfirst off the roof of his house, landing on his chest on a large basalt boulder. A specialist in traditional massage medicine was called in to treat his broken bones and hard and distended abdomen caused by internal injuries. While his family sat around crying over him, the massage specialist worked on him daily for nearly a week without any improvement. One week after his jump, Q was admitted to the hospital in critical condition. He had neither spoken nor eaten during this period. When I left Truk two and a half months later Q remained in the hospital in guarded condition.

CASE 11: AN INNOCENT VICTIM OF THE GAME OF DEATH

It was late afternoon one weekday, and the commuters were en route home to Peniyesene after a long day's work. Nearing the area between Tunnuuk and Peniyesene, the pickup in which H was riding slowed so that the riders could see what was happening off the road to the right. As H hunched forward to get a better look at a swirling fight involving a half dozen young men from Peniyesene and Söpwüük, he realized some of his close kinsmen were involved. Though he was by now an adult man and had recently taken a one-year *mwichen asor* pledge in an effort to curb his drinking, H was still young enough and confident enough in his own powers to rush to the aid of his kinsmen, who included two of his mother's brother's sons and a close lineage brother. As he endeavored to pull the fighters apart, a young berserker from Söpwüük stabbed him in the chest with a long knife. The blade entered a lung and severed a major artery, but H, gasping and clutching his wound, was able to stagger out to the road in search of a ride to the hospital. Since no vehicle was immediately forthcoming, he began walking toward town, bleeding all the while, until someone picked him up and rushed him to the medical center. By the time he reached the doctors, however, it was too late and he succumbed to massive internal bleeding and shock.[8] His killer was tried, found guilty, and sent to jail on Ponape to thwart the likelihood of revenge-motivated attempts on his life in Truk.

Despite the diversity of detail of the case studies presented above, certain common themes, listed below, can be seen.

1. While drunks are culturally defined as "insane," "out of control," and "beyond reason," it is clear that in most, if not all, instances, drunks can discriminate persons and contexts quite well and guide their craziness accordingly.
2. Nearly all drunken brawling is done by young men. Fighting provides an important sanctioned opportunity for them to demonstrate their bravery in public. Frequently drunkenness involves creating a public spectacle. The audience is an important, perhaps essential, part of this social drama.

3. One normally is not punished for drunken behavior. Anyone who interacts with a drunk does so at his or her own peril.
4. Being drunk permits one a variety of ways of expressing verbal and physical aggression against others.
5. Being drunk provides a major, legitimate excuse for the expression of intrafamily aggression (between parent and child, or between sibling and sibling). More typically, however, drunken aggression is directed outside the family in the form of interlineage or interdistrict warfare.
6. Drunk or sober, one ideally should go to the aid of a kinsman in distress even at the risk of one's own life.
7. Women and teenaged girls often joke with drunks, lead them home if they are related, and typically comprise a significant part of the audience to drunken performances.
8. When inebriated and interacting with Americans, drunks who typically avoid using English when sober may use it exclusively.[9]
9. Not all drunkenness ends in violence, but everyone is aware that the potential for an explosion is always present, and members of the audience remain alert for the subtle cues that indicate a swing in mood.
10. Drunkenness is an almost daily event in Peniyesene, and villagers expect to encounter inebriated young men at anytime and anyplace.

Men, Women, and Booze

5

The men on Truk occupy a social position so fraught with conflict and insecurity that even in the uninhibited relationship between sweethearts they are not able to express their hostility directly. They must, rather, turn a large part of it against themselves in the masochism which characterizes their participation in this relationship. The women of Truk, occupying as they do a more strongly supported social position than the men, are able to express their hostility more directly.

> J. L. Fischer and M. J. Swartz,
> "Socio-psychological aspects of
> some Trukese and Ponapean love
> songs"

MASCULINITY AND FEMININITY IN GREATER TRUKESE SOCIETY

From the first European descriptions of life in Greater Trukese Society, the extreme protectiveness of Trukese men toward their women has been a subject of comment. The Russian explorer Frederic Lütke, who lay over at Lukunor and Satawan in the Lower Mortlocks for a month in 1828 while conducting astronomical observations, was the first foreigner to write of this possessiveness (1835). Lütke and his sailors generally were denied any sight of Mortlockese women and were told to stay away from the areas they occupied. Only once during his visit was Lütke permitted to carry on a brief exchange with two girls. Lütke remained at a loss to explain this extraordinary defensiveness on the part of the men for their women and could only guess that it rose out of a concern for the women's general safety. Ten years later, in 1838, the French explorer Dumont d'Urville put into Truk Lagoon and went ashore with some of his men on Feefen Island. Finding the island men initially helpful and friendly, even though they were subsequently attacked by them, the Frenchmen were baffled when the few women they met fled screaming into the brush on their approach:

> Most of the females, one of the officers writes, must have been hidden away or whisked off to another island well in advance of the foreigners' coming. It was only after one of the Europeans prudently declined the offer of a village beauty for the evening on the grounds that he and his companion were under a tabu that women were permitted to approach him. This extreme solicitude on the part of Trukese men for their women does not, as has been argued, necessarily imply earlier unhappy experiences with foreign sailors, for Trukese are inclined to be protective of their females even today. [Hezel 1973a:59]

This "strong, protective current of feeling on the part of other members of their family" is offered by Akapito et al. (1975:8) as a major reason why most Trukese women do not frequent bars in the district center today.

Two major cultural notions regarding masculinity and femininity in Truk are revealed in the examples of protectiveness mentioned above. First, women generally are consigned to the private sphere while men represent them in public. Trukese view it as highly irregular and inappropriate for a woman to speak out or in other ways be assertive in the public realm. Hence women do not usually deliver speeches at public meetings, nor do they seek elective political office in Truk. Nearly all traditional political positions were filled by males. If a woman lacks a brother to defend her interests in public, she is pitied by others. Provision of a brother is a common motive for adoption of boys by parents who have only daughters (Marshall 1976b). Masculinity is public and assertive. Femininity is private and acquiescent.

The second cultural notion regarding masculinity and femininity has to do with elements of danger and risk. As noted in chapter 3, males in Greater Trukese Society are encouraged to meet and master danger— almost by definition, to be male is to learn to take risks and to laugh in the face of adversity. This belief finds expression in the value of bravery, but it comes out even more tellingly in the alternative name for strong thought: *ekiyekin mwään* 'manly thought'. Rightly or wrongly, women are generally believed to think *ekiyekin feefin* 'weak thoughts'.[1] Females are encouraged to avoid risks and to shun dangerous situations whenever possible. Strange foreign vessels and their equally strange looking crews must have been viewed by Trukese as dangerous and risky. Males mustered their courage and went forward to encounter this danger; females remained true to their gender by staying back and avoiding it. When danger intruded into the village in the persons of Europeans, women ran away from it. Only when assured that the Frenchmen represented no apparent threat did women on Feefen approach them; similarly, we can assume that Lütke was finally permitted a brief chat with Lukunor women near the end of his sojourn because he and his crew had minded their manners and posed no obvious danger to the islanders. In like fashion today, bars are looked upon as places of potential danger because of the frequent fights that erupt there; they are not thought proper places for women.

In a limited sense, Trukese infants of either sex are neuter. This is shown by the single term for infant, *monukön*. By the time they reach age 3 or 4, however, young children begin to be actively distinguished as boys and girls, and socialization for male and female roles begins. Youngsters continue to play in mixed groups throughout childhood, but as they approach their teens they increasingly begin to segregate themselves by sex. More or less coincident with the onset of puberty, boys and girls begin the transformation into the appropriate young adult category: *anuön* for 'young men' and *faapwin* for 'young women'. Public interactions with members of the opposite sex become more constrained and circumspect, even though young adults are expected to commence having private affairs with members of the opposite sex in their early teens.

Along with the increasing differentiation of the sexes by play groups and life-cycle categories goes a separation of work roles into those appropriate for males and those proper for females. Boys and young men begin to fish, climb coconut and breadfruit trees to harvest the fruit, and engage in other activities involving strength and potential risk. Girls and young women assist in food preparation,[2] child care, laundry, and other domestic chores. Boys learn to fight, while girls learn to sew. Boys run freely in groups roaming far from home, while girls stay close to home in the immediate village area. Boys and young men generally are given fewer responsibilities than their female counterparts and less is expected of them at this stage in life. If a young man fails to accomplish an assigned task or refuses to help because he "doesn't feel like it," this is accepted by parents. After all, "boys will be boys." For a young woman to show such irresponsibility, however, is a matter for great concern and very likely will result in a physical beating from her mother. Young women work hard whether they want to or not. Young men play hard whether their parents like it or not.

The role of the sexes in church affairs reveals much about cultural expectations of males and females. Leadership patterns in the church, with the sole exception of women's clubs, are vested entirely in men. Native pastors, and catechists, deacons, and other church officials are always males who have passed into full-fledged manhood. The congregation present for worship services always is overwhelmingly female. Most of the males present are small boys accompanying their mothers and sisters.[3] It is considered an important virtue for young women and adult women to be *soulang* 'saintly' or 'Christian'. This identity involves regular attendance at scheduled church services, active participation in church women's affairs (e.g., choir or service clubs), not smoking tobacco, and total abstinence from alcoholic beverages. Just as a young man obtains and defends his public reputation through acts of derring-do, young women prove themselves proper and desirable marriage partners by involving themselves in church activities and by avoiding the use of alcohol and tobacco. These latter substances have thus become an important indicator of sexual identity and of religious commitment in Greater Trukese Society today.[4]

Because young men "must" use tobacco and liquor, few of them are considered to be *soulang*. In fact, to be saintly would be a denial of their manhood at this stage in their lives. Quite predictably, then, most Peniyesene young men avoid attending church services entirely. As young men become adult men they are expected to moderate their use of alcohol. Those men who aspire to the highly coveted positions of church leadership must completely abstain from spiritous drink. Despite the fulminations of the early missionaries against tobacco use by Christians in Truk, it has now become acceptable for men who are *soulang* to smoke. Such men are not encouraged to smoke, however, and they command greater respect when they do not. It is believed that females who are *soulang* absolutely should not smoke.

Male and female are fundamentally opposite categories in the Trukese conception of things (figure 15). This opposition may be summarized as follows:

Male	Female
Public	Private
Assertive	Acquiescent
Confronts danger	Shuns danger
Takes risks	Avoids risks
Right hand/strength	Left hand/weakness
Strong thought	Weak thought
Should smoke tobacco	Should not smoke tobacco
Should drink liquor	Should not drink liquor

This basic opposition between the sexes is elaborated on below, with an eye toward showing how it affects the nature of alcohol use in Greater Trukese Society.[5]

Figure 15. Young men and women of Peniyesene

POOLHALL AS MEN'S HOUSE

Widespread throughout Micronesian societies are large, beautifully crafted, A-frame structures referred to variously as canoe houses or men's houses. Although the specific activities that take place in these structures vary from culture to culture in Micronesia, these buildings are commonly used predominantly by males. In Truk Lagoon, men's houses are called *uut* (Mortlockese *fääl*), and they serve as dormitories for the young men of the lineage who have to leave their parental dwellings at puberty to avoid sleeping under the same roof as their sisters. *Uut* also are the site of lineage meetings, a place in which to entertain visitors (usually males) from other districts or islands, a place to store canoes and fishing gear, and the locus for a variety of ritual and social activities. Traditionally, every lineage erected a men's house on its homesite, and this building was where raids and warfare were planned and plotted against neighboring groups.

A few men's houses remain in Peniyesene today, but not every lineage has one anymore. A great many of the activities formerly carried out in men's houses no longer take place there, if they take place at all. In this altered situation, the village poolhall in Peniyesene has taken on a special significance for young men as a kind of modern day equivalent of the *uut*. Like traditional men's houses, the poolhall may be entered by women only at certain times and with a proper show of "respect." The poolhall is masculine "turf."

Recall that the poolhall consists of one-half of a single large room, the other half of which is a village store (see figure 8). Persons may enter this room from the outside through two doors, one on the store side and the other on the side of the poolhall. Normally, eight or ten young men may be found lounging around the pool table on rude wooden benches watching some of their number gamble at *tamatsuki*, the Japanese loan word Trukese use for pocket billiards. Boys begin at age 11 or 12 to practice pool when the table is not occupied by older youths. By the time they reach their twenties most young men in Truk are extremely skilled at this game. In addition to the young men kibbitzers, one or two older men and a scattering of young boys fill out the audience.

Adult women and teenaged girls are almost never found sitting around the pool table, and they never play at this game. They and male informants unanimously concur that it would be *aseu* 'embarrassing' 'shameful' for them to do so.[6] I once observed a young woman from Mwään village, the wife of a Peniyesene youth, sitting brazenly in the poolhall alongside her husband, to the notable discomfort of several others present. When postpubescent females enter the poolhall/store, they usually take the door farthest from the pool table. Failing that, they slip quickly through the other door and move straight toward the store counter, eyes averted and bent slightly at the waist in a show of respect. Generally, women avoid even looking at the pool game and its audience while they make their purchases. They leave quickly in the same way they came in.

In contemporary Truk, playing pool, like pounding breadfruit, is considered men's work, but this does not explain why women avoid the poolhall. This *nenien mwään* 'men's place' is a spot where males congregate to gossip, banter, tell off-color jokes, and generally let their hair down. The presence of women inhibits all these activities since nearly any woman who entered would be a sister of one of the men, in whose presence everyone must carefully avoid reference to anything having to do with sex, elimination and the like. Women also stay away from the pool hall because it is a favorite hangout for weekend warriors. Drunks regularly relax in the poolhall or drop in to see what is going on. In addition, many fights break out in or near the poolhall, which is adjacent to the village battleground. The poolhall is therefore viewed by women as a dangerous place, to be shunned when possible.

Akapito et al. (1975:8) suggest that many Trukese view the downtown bars on Moen as similar to traditional men's meeting houses. I agree that they serve this function, among many others, for bar drinkers. But it must be kept in mind that most drinking in Truk takes place elsewhere than in the downtown bars, which are the havens of the monied elite. Since all suburban villages like Peniyesene lack bars but many have poolhalls, I suggest that the poolhall is for the boonie drinker what the tavern is for the bar drinker—a meeting house where men can publicly come together more or less undisturbed by their wives and other female kin. Not only has the fearless Trukese warrior switched from coconut to rum and coke, he has also substituted poolhalls for the traditional men's houses.

WHY WOMEN DO NOT DRINK

The foregoing discussion suggests that there must be some basic, underlying reason why more than nine out of ten Trukese women never even taste alcoholic beverages, much less drink them on a regular basis.[7] The central position of women in Trukese family life is crucial to understanding why women and alcohol are not allowed to mix in Truk. Alcohol is defined by Trukese as a substance that leads to temporary insanity; drunks become irresponsible persons. But women are responsible first and foremost for home and hearth. They tend small children, cook the food, wash the dishes and the laundry, gather firewood, and perform myriad other jobs of utmost importance to the basic maintenance of family life and human survival. Unlike most masculine tasks associated with food-getting activities and the domestic routine, women's work cannot usually be ignored or put off for long. A sick child demands attention. A new infant must be nursed. A hungry family requires feeding. Were a woman to go out drinking and carousing and subsequently become "irresponsible," what would become of all these essential duties? Frequent drunkenness on the part of large numbers of Trukese women would lead to the collapse of domestic life. From the Trukese viewpoint, this simply cannot be allowed. On the other hand, frequent drunkenness by males—primarily young men—does not threaten the operation of essential social machinery and can therefore be tolerated. For these reasons young women are told repeatedly that they must eschew liquor at all costs.[8]

MANHOOD AND MACHISMO

The concept of *machismo*, which derives from the Spanish ideal of manliness, is the art of displaying manly superiority. The "macho" male achieves his sexual identity by dominating others with his wits and fists, must be ready to defend his honor even at the risk of death, and seeks to exercise complete authority over the women in his life (Madsen and Madsen 1969:712). A macho male strives to pile up numerous sexual conquests outside of marriage. Young boys growing up in cultures where *machismo* is held up as ideal masculine behavior quickly learn by observation that in the struggle for superiority it is the aggressive male who wins out. They also learn to expect aggression and hostility from others.

In the Mexican version of *machismo*, drinking liquor frequently and in quantity is viewed as a basic means of displaying virility. Abstinence from alcohol by males indicates a lack of *machismo* and is negatively valued. In a study of drinking behavior in a Mexican village, Maccoby (1972) discovered *machismo* to be directly correlated with aggressiveness and belligerency and inversely correlated with ratings of responsibility, cooperation, satisfaction in work, and general productivity. This association between *machismo* and belligerency comes out very clearly in the following quote from Madsen and Madsen:

> Mexicans admire the person "with balls" as we say. . . . The one who has guts enough to stand up against an older and stronger guy is more respected. . . . If any so-and-so comes up to me and says, "Fuck your mother," I answer, "Fuck your mother a thousand times." And if he gives one step forward and I take one step back, I lose prestige. But if I go forward too, and pile on and make a fool of him, then others will treat me with respect. In a fight I would never give up or say, "Enough," even though the other was killing me. I would try to go to my death smiling. That is what we mean by being "macho." [1969:715]

Maccoby attributes this aggressiveness to a basic masculine insecurity masked by a show of bravado and presumed superiority over women. He goes on to argue that the Mexican male's *machismo* "is a reaction to his fear of women, a compensation for his feelings of weakness, dependence, and passivity" (1972:247). Maccoby also asserts that Mexicans indulge male irresponsibility and impulsiveness while expecting women to be *abnegada* 'self-sacrificing' and to bear greater burdens than men without complaint. Madsen (1964) describes the Latin female as taking on the perfect counterpart or antithetic role to her man: she should be sexually pure, weak, and respectful of her husband's wishes. Her life should center in the home and family while her "lord and master" represents them to the outside world. Mexican men try to be the living validation of the premise that males are stronger, more reliable, and of greater intelligence than

89

women. They are almost obsessively engaged in maintaining a public image of independence, honor, and self-reliance.

Machismo is also found in some Mediterranean societies where many of the features just described for Mexico also occur. For example, in Yugoslavia, the ability to consume vast amounts of liquor is a highly valued trait. "Real men" are those who drink often and heavily (Simic 1969). The bravado that accompanies drinking may lead to violence when one cannot retreat without loss of face. Although males are thought to possess the strength and stamina required to withstand the effects of hard drinking, "the more fragile nature of women precludes intoxicating distillants as a threat to their integrity" (Simic 1969:97). Simic concludes that the apparently irrational or unproductive behavior of some Yugoslav men can be at least partially explained in terms of anxieties wrought by an inability to match up to ideal standards of male excellence: "As in Mexico, the qualities of 'manliness' are stressed and there is considerable concern regarding the face presented to the outside world. In response to these preoccupations the culture has provided socially sanctioned patterns of action which dramatically portray the elements of machismo" (1969:100). Whether we speak of Mexico, Yugoslavia, or other countries in which macho behavior flourishes, the points made above in describing *machismo* also apply right down the line to males in Greater Trukese Society.

Trukese males exhibit an exaggerated concern with their physical capacity. Although they will suffer injuries with stoicism and even pride (see, e.g., chapter 4, case 8), they retire meekly and resignedly to their beds at the first sign of illness (Gladwin 1953:308). Trukese women are expected to react violently and openly to grief, but the macho Trukese male should remain in stony silence, permitting himself only a quiet tear if he is especially moved (Gladwin and Sarason 1953:157). Trukese men attach great importance to sexual adequacy as a reflection of personal adequacy. Out of a need to prove themselves strong masculine figures, Trukese males strive to conquer women sexually to show assertiveness (Gladwin and Sarason 1953:113, 230, 233). Echoing Maccoby's description of the Mexican male's fear of women, which is grounded in dependence on them, Gladwin and Sarason maintain that "the Trukese male feels dependent upon women, strives hard to win and maintain their attention, is submissive toward them, and is unable or unwilling to express toward them his deep feelings of hostility and resentment" (1953:233). All of this leads to what Frances Caughey has called the "paradoxical status" of men on Truk: "socially they are held to be 'higher' than women, and respect and obedience are their just due, but individually each man is in a subservient position to his wife's lineage" (1971:5).

The personal reputation carried by every Trukese male is not unlike the concept of *honor* or *face* found in countries where *machismo* is a dominant masculine value.[9] We have already noted the quickness with which Trukese men move to defend their honor in public confrontations, and we have seen that the drunken battles among young men may be interpreted as a struggle for superiority in which the aggressive (but respectful) male wins out. Like the proverbial Latin lovers, the Trukese male strives to engage in a long string of extramarital sexual conquests over women as a show of virility. Fathering many children, whether in or out of wedlock, is viewed as a sign of strength by Trukese men. Along these same lines, a man traditionally could demonstrate his personal power by possessing more than one wife, although Christian teachings have now put an end to polygyny in Truk. Having more than one wife "showed that a man was of such unusual capacity that he could take on several burdensome social relationships at the same time or, better, that he was able to turn what was customarily a subordinate relationship to another lineage into an equal or dominant one" (Caughey 1970:226).

Drinking often and with abandon is highly valued among young men in Truk; not to drink is negatively valued by Trukese males because abstinence indicates an unwillingness to face risks, to play the game of death, to be macho. Trukese indulge and even encourage irresponsibility and impulsiveness in young men, and Trukese women, like their Latin counterparts, take on the perfect antithetic role to their hard-drinking, aggressive, macho men.

As Gladwin has shown, the outward, public dominance of Trukese men over women turns out to be a chimera on closer inspection:

> An anthropologist or any other foreigner in contact with the Trukese is immediately impressed by the degree to which the men are dominant in the society. One quickly becomes convinced that the women are subservient, insecure, and afraid to express themselves in the presence of their lords and masters. Granted there are occasional episodes which may give one pause in regard to this stereotype but they are overwhelmed by the weight of contrary, though superficial, evidence. Thus, it is a man who heads the household group, and the oldest man in the lineage . . . is the final arbiter of the affairs of its members. All political power and most esoteric knowledge is in the hands of men. In the adulterous liaisons which seem to preoccupy most Trukese during their active adult years, it is always the man who takes the initiative. . . . Breadfruit is the most important staple food of the Trukese . . . and its collection and preparation is almost exclusively a male task. . . . Men beat their wives with impunity and in general extend to them little consideration and few courtesies. It is perhaps justifiable in the light of this array of evidence that, after four years of constant association with the Trukese, I still brought back with me the belief that the man is in a securely dominant position in the society.

91

> Then Dr. Sarason analyzed the Rorschachs, and after them
> the TAT's, and in both cases concluded that the men were notably
> more anxious than the women and would tend to respond less
> adequately in any situation of conflict or doubt. [Gladwin
> 1953:306-7]

Still unconvinced that men were not clearly dominant, Gladwin returned
to his own ethnographic material to see whether on reexamination support could be found for Sarason's conclusions. On doing so he found that
"Dr. Sarason's hypothesis of masculine insecurity is not only plausible
but throws into clear perspective the greater problems of adjustment
faced by the Trukese man compared to the woman as they grow to ma-
turity in their society" (Gladwin 1953:307). This insecurity of males relative to females in Greater Trukese Society can be attributed to the
greater difficulties young men face in meeting cultural expectations for
manliness, a dilemma that perfectly mirrors the situation faced by macho
males in Yugoslavia.

Trukese men spend a lot of time convincing themselves and visitors
among them of their superiority over women. They boss women about in
aggressive tones and expect their wives or sisters to do a host of menial
tasks for them whenever they demand it. They emphasize how much
stronger men are than women and they boast of their greater capacity for
reason, deliberation, and general intellectual endeavor. As a rule they
consider themselves much more intelligent than women. This is a major
reason why, until very recently, few women were permitted education
beyond the elementary level by their families. The few highly educated
young women from Truk who have obtained a college education in recent
years are viewed by many men as threatening because they have proved
themselves better or more learned. At the same time, these women are
sought for wives as "prized catches" because of their potential wage-earn-
ing capacity.[10] Trukese men think of themselves as responsible and reliable; they stereotype their women as scatterbrained emotional persons
unfit to cope with weighty political or economic matters. Again we find
a direct correlate of these Trukese male beliefs in the concept of *machismo:* "Machismo indicates an attitude of male superiority, a wish to
control women and keep them in an inferior position" (Maccoby 1972:246).

Finally, the aggressiveness described above for Mexican males operating according to the tenets of *machismo* also exists in Greater Trukese
Society (see chapter 4, cases 1, 2, 3, 6, 7, and 9). This pattern of drunken
assertiveness has even been carried by Trukese to Ponape in their home-
stead settlements there. Writing about the Piis-Losap community in Me-
talanihm on Ponape, Severance has observed that "the three or four
occasions of known alcohol use during my stay . . . twice led to overt
aggressive behavior with the common Trukese motif, 'Come, are you [a]

man?! I will take your life now', interspersed with apologies for [sic] the kinsmen who were trying to quiet and calm the individual and his nurtured grievance" (1974:14).

In American culture one way to put a man down is to accuse him of being a sissy or womanlike. Similarly, Americans denigrate the "pushy," aggressive, masculine woman. The same sort of thing goes on in Trukese culture. For instance, women on Wuumaan Island reportedly should have two important tools of work: the *epino* 'hand net for fishing' and the *säwa* 'fishing basket', and "a woman who lacks them may be sneered at as being 'like a man'" (Caughey 1970:xix). Likewise, to be a man in Truk means to possess certain tools such as a machete, breadfruit-cutting pole, carrying basket, breadfruit scraper, pounder, and pounding board. A man who lacks these tools "is seen as 'like a woman' (only a woman lacks such tools)" (Caughey 1970:69). Moreover, the ultimate masculine put-down in Truk used "to insult another as one who is weak and womanly in his thinking . . . [is to] . . . say '[Go] wear a woman's clothes'" (Caughey 1970:45). Interestingly, young men who drink and fight only in their own village are deprecated as women by other young men. I was told that real men drink and fight away from their home turf, either in uninhabited areas, in other villages, or in the downtown bars. These places are all considered more dangerous because the drinker is much less likely to find others who will rush to his aid or intervene to break up a fight in which he may get involved. We see, then, that Trukese men must work hard to avoid seeming womanly, and Trukese women must refrain from appearing macho. And, of course, a major means for showing off one's *machismo* in Truk is to consume liquor in copious amounts. A Trukese woman who drinks would be acting like a man.

Not only do Latin women play a demure counterpoint to their macho male relatives, but they also step in when necessary to lead a man home. Describing a mestizo village in Oaxaca, Dennis discusses the nonformalized feminine role as follows: "They are quick to lead away an inebriated male relative, put him quietly to sleep, perhaps cajole him into leaving a situation which is becoming unpleasant. A women plays a sort of corollary role, that of guardian of the drunk. She is expected to enforce respect for social norms, and to manage her stronger but less responsible male relatives" (1975:858). Precisely the same role exists for Trukese women vis-à-vis their male kin (see chapter 4, cases 1, 4 and 9). Time and again in Peniyesene I watched sisters lead their drunken brothers home by the hand, or I observed wives constrain their husbands from jumping into the fray when a fight threatened or was already under way. I also heard of at least two cases where Peniyesene wives, irked by their husbands' heavy drinking, got hold of their husbands' drinking permits and tore them up. On other occasions in Peniyesene I saw women swipe bottles of liquor from their inebriated male relatives when the latter were not looking. All these activities on the part of women can be seen as part of their attempt to play guardian of the drunk.

DEALING WITH DRUNKS

We have just noted that women often watch over drunken male relatives in the village setting, but once a man is involved in a brawl women do not try to intervene directly. Moreover, it is considered inappropriate for them to lecture at or scold drunks. When they do so, this typically stimulates the drunk to new acts of violence (see, e.g., chapter 4, cases 3 and 4). How, then, do Trukese deal with fighting drunks? And who, if anyone, may step in to restrain physically or punish a drunken man?

The normal way sober persons of any age and either sex deal with drunks is to not deal with them—that is, avoidance is considered the wisest strategy when a drunk is observed lurching about (cf. Dennis 1975). If one cannot avoid a drunk, then one must be careful not to annoy him. Speaking softly and soothingly, agreeing with whatever inanity he may utter, providing him with whatever he may demand (e.g., food or cigarettes), and getting away as quickly as possible without appearing to flee are considered the best ways to avoid antagonizing a drunk. These rules of thumb should be especially honored by women, children, and the parents of the drunk. Sober males may choose to interact with drunks, but they always do so at their own peril (see, e.g., chapter 4, case 11). The only persons who may forcefully confront a drunk (other than fellow drunks, of course) are the individual's brothers. Although a brother may strike his drunken sibling, he is nonetheless at risk of being attacked since the strong cultural proscription against aggression among siblings is dissolved by ethanol (see, e.g., chapter 4, cases 3, 4, 5, 10, 11). Despite the role of women as guardians of their intoxicated male relatives, women usually stay clear of drunks to whom they are not related. The reason given for this by men and women alike is that women fear being beaten by drunks and, among many other things, the state of drunkenness does permit men to strike women.

Whenever possible, then, drunks are to be shunned by sober persons even though their actions may be watched with amusement, irritation, or even horror from a safe distance. At the approach of a drunk, sensible women and children run away. Although sober males do not actually run from a drunk (to do so would undermine their own reputation for manliness), they may try to disappear nonchalantly from his line of attention.

LOVE, SEX, AND AGGRESSION

Having by now a reasonably good understanding of what it means to be a man or a woman in Truk, we are in a position to consider one of the major arenas in which the battle of the sexes is fought: the sweetheart relationship. Trukese young men and women are recognized to be preoccupied with sex, and this is given as a reason why they do not begin to learn esoteric lore until their middle to late thirties (Goodenough 1949). This preoccupation with sex finds its major expression in extramarital affairs wherein "intercourse is often likened to a contest in which the partner who first achieves an orgasm is said to lose to the other. The men say that a woman may laugh at a man if he fails to satisfy her" (Goodenough 1949:619).[11]

Not only does a man who fails to bring a woman to orgasm lose to her, but he must also undergo the further indignity of derision: "In one standard insult phrase the girl will advise the man who lost to 'take the breast' since he is incompetent 'like a baby' (*wussun monukön*)" (Caughey 1970:202). Once more we encounter the Trukese stress on proving oneself competent through successful performance, and once again we see that it is the man, more than the woman, who must so prove himself. Not only must a man demonstrate sexual adequacy by not losing to his lover, but the deck is stacked against him to begin with. Goodenough (1949:619) notes that the physical conditions under which clandestine intercourse frequently takes place are "stressful" and impair the probability of the woman reaching orgasm. In Gladwin's phrase, intercourse is a contest in which "it is only the man who can lose and not the woman" (1953:308). In sex, as in everything else, the Trukese man must take risks if he is to prove himself competent. And wherever risks are taken, the possibility of failure always looms in the background.

A good deal of aggression rises to the surface in the competitive love affairs of Trukese young people. While their sweetheart relationship is risky, it appears to offer more genuine satisfaction to Trukese than the marital bed, and it is the only sexual relationship in which Trukese feel free to let themselves go. As one way of demonstrating one's undying devotion to the partner, it is common to engage in mutual mutilation. The scars that result are worn with pride as a symbol of sexual conquest by young men (cf. chapter 4, case 8), and they represent evidence of what the lovers are willing to endure for each other (Swartz 1958:478). These "acts of love" are perpetrated in several different ways:

> Scarification was, and still is, practiced by young men who desire to prove their love to a sweetheart. The operation, termed *nekenek*, consists in making one or more cuts on the arm or chest with a knife (formerly a sharp piece of shell). In some cases these cuts are rubbed with the sap from the skin of a papaya, said to cause slow healing and formation of scar tissue.
> During coital foreplay either partner may scratch the other on the side of the neck or on the buttocks with the fingernails, this

practice being termed *nömuti*. Under the same circumstances the glowing end of a cigarette butt may be used by either partner on the arms or chest of the other, a practice termed *kek;* formerly the glowing end of a coconut leaflet midrib was used in the same way, the process then being termed *niköpwöt*. [LeBar 1964:171].

The pain inflicted on each other by sweethearts is now mostly limited to cigarette burns on the arm, but formerly included cutting with a knife and knocking out teeth with stones. It is a mutual expression of both in-turned and out-turned aggression. [Swartz 1958:482]

Young men subject themselves to this scarification much more frequently than young women (Gladwin and Sarason 1953:111; Swartz 1958:483). Swartz (1958) argues that this reveals a masochistic streak in Trukese males, but I would add that it also provides yet one more avenue for young men to show bravery by submitting to pain without flinching or making outcry.

Beyond cigarette burns and other similar expressions of devotion, additional aggression comes out within the sweetheart relationship itself. This is in the form of what has been referred to in the literature as "Trukese striking" (*wechewechen Chuuk*). Swartz (1958) says that his informants viewed this practice as the best way to bring a woman quickly to orgasm. The word *wech* 'hit' 'strike', which is reduplicated as *wechewech* to show repetition and duration, in this context refers to the man repeatedly prodding his partner's clitoris with his erect penis until she reaches an ecstatic orgasm. Done skillfully, this technique requires no penetration at all. As Swartz observes, "the man is 'striking' the woman in a kind of competition in which, if he loses by not 'striking' adequately enough to bring orgasm, he must pay the penalty of being laughed at; this is something the Trukese dislike intensely" (1958:481).

In his provocative article on the sweetheart relationship, Swartz (1958) concludes that men more than women deal with their aggressive feelings by turning them inward upon themselves. Along these lines of masochistic masculine aggression in Truk it is worth recalling that the vast majority of suicides in Greater Trukese Society likewise involve males rather than females (see chapter 4, case 10 and Hezel 1976). I submit that drunkenness may be profitably viewed as an extension of this proclivity for male masochism. While drunk, young men quite frequently get reprimanded by elder kinsmen, thrown in jail, beaten up, wounded, and occasionally even killed. All this inward aggression is brought on voluntarily by assuming the social identity of the drunk. Young male Trukese drunks prove their courage as much by their ability to withstand pain resulting from masochistic exposure to danger as by overt aggressive acts against others.

ON BEING A MAN IN TRUK: SOME SUMMARY COMMENTS

In Greater Trukese Society, gender is ascribed at birth, but a positive, valued sexual identity as a "manly" or "womanly" person must be achieved by both sexes. In the course of becoming masculine or feminine, that is in living up to Trukese culture's ideals of masculinity and femininity, males must always work much harder, run greater risks of failure, and operate under more psychological stress than females. This stress reaches a crescendo for young men.

Alcohol use aids in the process of becoming manly in a variety of ways. It serves as a symbol of age-group identity, clearly demarcating young men from boys, who do not drink liquor (figure 16). Use of intoxicating drinks also clearly sets young men apart from young women, as we have already seen. The drunken behaviors characteristic of young men—audacious, obnoxious, and aggressive as they may be—are a culturally sanctioned means for allowing young men to demonstrate prowess and prove their manhood in physical combat. Being able to drink a lot of alcohol is looked upon as a sign of strength, which is in turn a further validation of manhood. In this sense, alcohol use joins a host of other behaviors and carefully cultivated personal characteristics that publicly display virility.

For a healthy self-image, young men in Truk must enter the adult man category believing themselves physically able and competent to deal successfully in risky situations. They must begin to develop verbal skill or strength as orators, show their learnedness by mastering the formal educational system and/or the wage employment sector of the economy, and begin to sire children and have a number of successful love affairs from which they emerge the winners. Success in sweetheart relationships hinges importantly on a male's attractiveness to members of the opposite sex. Such attractiveness is tremendously enhanced by a reputation for bravery (Caughey 1970:202). Drunken brawling by young men while the young ladies look on provides the most convenient and readily available contemporary stage from which to show off their charms to potential sweethearts.[12]

For a young man in Truk to fail to drink liquor would be unthinkable for all of these reasons. His identity as a maturing male would be placed in jeopardy, his opportunities for proving his masculinity would be substantially reduced, the likelihood he would be publicly derided by his peers for behaving like a woman would be very high, and his chances for success with the young ladies would be next to nil. Given this central importance of alcohol in the process of becoming a man in contemporary Truk, we can now turn our attention to several social scientific explanations for why people drink differently in different societies.

Media Class, Xavier High School, Truk

Figure 16. Some weekend warriors
from Peniyesene

98

Anxiety,
Social Organization,
Dependency, and Power:
Why Do Trukese Drink?

6

We maintain that drinking behavior is mainly a
reflection of traditional forms of social organization
and cultural values instead of a reflection of social
disorganization.

J. Levy and S. J. Kunitz, Indian
Drinking: Navajo Practices and
Anglo-American Theories

INTRODUCTORY COMMENTS

Over the years that alcohol use and abuse have occupied the attention of
social scientists, a number of different theories have been proposed to
account for cross-cultural variation in the amount of liquor consumed and
in the radical differences observed in peoples' drunken comportment. We
examine below the four most influential of these theories to see how well
each explains weekend warfare in Truk.

ANXIETY

What has come to be known in the literature as "anxiety theory" in regard
to the differential use of alcoholic beverages derives from Horton's (1943)

seminal paper on the functions of alcohol in primitive societies. In this paper Horton argued that the primary function of alcoholic beverages in all societies is to cause drunkenness, which reduces anxiety brought on by (a) precarious subsistence and/or (b) acculturation. Horton classified a sample of fifty-six societies according to the degree of insobriety they displayed and the level of anxiety that appeared to exist among their members.[1] He then demonstrated statistically that the degree of drunkenness increased hand in hand with the degree of anxiety—that is, anxiety is the motive for drinking. Honigmann (1973:253) refers to Horton's approach as "the prevalent conception in the anthropology of heavy drinking."

Horton's approach assumes that persons are filled with drives that are held in check only by culturally learned inhibitions. In this view, disinhibited behavior results from the release of repressed drives. Disinhibited acts are usually punished, and Horton reasons that individuals will try to avoid punishment and will be anxious over releasing their repressed drives for fear of punishment. Beverage alcohol is looked upon as a disinhibitor that strips away the thin veneer of learned inhibitions, reducing a person to a state in which the baser instincts, such as aggressive and sexual impulses, break into the open. Thus Horton's approach presumes that drinkers consume alcohol to reduce anxieties. In circumstances where release of inhibited responses is not punished, anxieties are reduced by disinhibition. The positive rewards derived from the actualization of inhibited impulses in combination with reduced anxieties "should serve to give the drinking habit extraordinary strength" (1943:227).

Actually, Horton's idea was a bit more complex than indicated above. He noted that it is not sufficient to assume the amount of drinking that goes on is directly proportional to the "strength of the anxiety drive in any case" because drinking itself may raise new anxieties:

> If the reduction of anxiety by alcohol permits formerly inhibited sexual or aggressive responses to occur, and if these are punished; or if it is followed by the immediately painful consequences of failure of physiological functions, then anxiety as an anticipation of these punishments may become attached to the act of drinking, or to any of the acts related to drinking, including the sight of liquor or the thought of it. The anxiety-reducing function of alcohol will then be opposed by its anxiety-arousing effect. These antagonistic responses will produce a dilemma situation in which a modification of the drinking response will be learned. In short, the actual, observed drinking habit will have to take the competing responses into account. [1943:223–24]

From this Horton concluded that societies that heavily punish aggressive and sexual responses by drinkers will raise these secondary anxieties for those who drink, and that this will either inhibit or eradicate the drinking response. On the other hand, if the original anxieties that motivated drinking are strong and society does not punish or only mildly punishes antisocial drinking behavior, then drinking will be reinforced.

Against this background, Horton set out to test the validity of three theorems and four corollaries:

Theorems:
1. The drinking of alcohol tends to be accompanied by the release of sexual and aggressive impulses.
2. The strength of the drinking response in any society tends to vary directly with the level of anxiety in that society.
3. The strength of the drinking response tends to vary inversely with the strength of the counteranxiety elicited by painful experiences during and after drinking.

Corollaries. The sources of such painful experiences are:
a. Actualization of real dangers as a result of impairment of physiological functions.
b. Social punishments for impairment of functions.
c. Social punishments invoked by the release of sexual response.
d. Social punishments invoked by the release of aggressive responses. [1943:230]

On the surface, the anxiety theory has a kind of plausibility that makes it appealing as an explanation of why people drink. On closer examination, however, this plausibility decreases and Horton's theory is not adequate to explain the durability and meaning of the drinking custom.

Horton first measured anxiety for the societies in his sample according to their dominant food-getting or subsistence activity on the assumption

> that the more primitive a society's food-getting techniques, the greater the danger of food shortage, [and] the more difficult the conditions of life generally. Under such conditions anxiety should be high. Where food-getting techniques are less primitive, the greater is the chance that conditions of food security may prevail. Under these conditions anxiety may be relatively low. [1943:263]

With this idea in mind Horton classified societies into five categories: hunting, herding, lower agriculture, intermediate agriculture, and higher agriculture. Hunting societies were presumed to have the most precarious subsistence base, and those with higher agriculture were believed to have the greatest subsistence security.[2] On this scale, Greater Trukese Society can be characterized as "lower agriculture," which Horton defines "as a subsistence economy in which agriculture is coordinate with hunting or fishing, or both, and herding is absent" (1943:264). Knowing this we would expect the Trukese to have only an average or moderate subsistence anxiety.

In fact, aboriginally, the islands of Greater Trukese Society were plagued by periodic food shortages, particularly on the outer island atolls, which had fewer resources than the high islands of Truk Lagoon and were more exposed to the ravages of the periodic typhoons that sweep through this part of the Pacific.[3] Even in the absence of a genuine shortage of food, Trukese evince a constant anxiety that borders on fetishism over food. Although their lands and lagoons normally provide them with plenty of food, the cultural meanings attached to food and the ways food is used in rewarding and punishing both children and adults make it a source of great concern to everyone: "The only time that one can imagine a Trukese completely without concern over food is in the presence of a large supply, already prepared, when his belly is so full he can eat no more" (Gladwin and Sarason 1953:250).

The second measure of anxiety Horton employed in his study concerns acculturation pressures. Although he set out initially to show the relationship between means of subsistence and styles of drinking, Horton ended his study by concluding that "a reliable positive association has been demonstrated between insobriety and subsistence hazards; a still more reliable positive association, when acculturation is included in the anxiety scale; and a 1:1 correspondence, between strong insobriety and acculturation" (1943:279). In discussing acculturation, Horton failed to provide a set of categories comparable to those he used to classify societies by mode of subsistence. A group was viewed either as acculturated or unacculturated. Matters of degree and criteria used in making these judgments were left to the reader's imagination.

By almost any measure the inhabitants of Greater Trukese Society have been subjected to strong acculturative influences over the past century. These influences include four different colonial powers, a major world war, and the introduction of ardent spirits (see chapter 2). Almost everyone familiar with the islands agrees that present-day acculturation—especially in the Micronesian port towns—is at an all-time high. Consequently, it is safe to assume that Greater Trukese Society would rank high on any scale of the relative degree of acculturation. According to Horton's theory, it follows that Trukese should be very anxious about contemporary outside influences and thus should drink heavily.

Anxiety wrought by acculturation has been used by Mahoney (1974) in an effort to explain "the possible link between alcohol and violent crime" in the Trust Territory. Averaging statistics on violent crimes and populations for Micronesia's six administrative districts from 1966 through

1972, Mahoney produces ratios of one violent crime per x thousand persons as follows:

Yap District	1:	1,236
Palau District	1:	2,128
Truk District	1:	2,466
Marianas District	1:	9,343
Ponape District	1:	11,284
Marshalls District	1:	48,675

He notes that the contrast between the first three and last three ratios is heightened by the fact that two of the three districts low in violent crimes (the Marianas and the Marshalls) "were consistently among the largest importers of alcoholic beverages at least between the years 1969 and 1972" (1974:23). Mahoney tries to explain this apparent anomaly by contending that the three high-crime districts "were the last parts of Micronesia to have sustained acculturative contact with the Western world, not really beginning until the last quarter of the nineteenth century" (1974:22). He then mentions the lengthy Spanish influence in the Marianas over the span of three centuries and maintains that "both the Marshalls and Ponape appear to have had some fifty years longer exposure to Western influence than Yap, Palau and Truk" (1974:23). This stretches the facts beyond the breaking point to fit the acculturation theory.

First, if we are to accept that violent crime rates are directly linked to drunkenness and that both decrease in proportion to length of culture contact with the West, then we should expect to find the Marianas with the lowest ratio of violent crimes. Clearly, this is not the case.[4] Second, it is difficult to know what Mahoney has chosen to recognize as "exposure to Western influence." By any measure, be it initial discovery, missionization, or resident traders, the Marshall Islands have not had "some fifty years longer exposure" than Yap, Palau, and Truk. The discoveries of all of these islands by European explorers took place over the course of 300 years or more.[5] Rather intensive archival investigation shows that imported trade alcohol did not become available in the Marshalls, Yap, or Palau until the 1870s, and in Truk until nearly the 1890s (Marshall and Marshall 1975). Acculturation anxiety fails to explain why Marianas drinkers commit a moderate, and not the smallest, number of violent crimes of Micronesia's peoples. It also fails to explain why Marshallese drinkers commit the fewest such crimes by a factor of 4.

Anxiety theory by itself falls down as an explanation for why Trukese drink as they do. It does not adequately handle subsistence anxiety over food and eating in this cultural setting, and Mahoney's efforts to use anxiety theory as an explanation for differences in drunken comportment and crime rates among Micronesian peoples do not convince the critical reader. Evidently, something else must account for the incidence and nature of alcohol use in Truk.

SOCIAL ORGANIZATION

Perhaps the answer to why Trukese imbibe as they do can be found by examining the social organization of Greater Trukese Society. In his reassessment of Horton's findings, Field (1962) used the same sample of fifty-six societies to reach rather different conclusions. He argued that acculturation does not necessarily increase anxiety; on the contrary, it may in fact reduce anxiety by "diminishing supernatural fears, or by providing rational solutions for anxiety-arousing cultural problems" (1962:57). Field claimed that acculturation actually disorganizes and destroys the social structure, a process which he felt is facilitated by "an originally loose tribal social organization": "For these reasons, it seems reasonable to suppose that Horton's relation between drunkenness and acculturation indicates an underlying process of loosening of a traditional social organization, not increased anxiety" (1962:57–58). But here Field's interpretation encounters its first impasse in the Trukese data: traditional lineage organization remains strong and viable in Truk and does not appear to have "loosened" in response to foreign intrusion.

Field's research reconfirmed Horton's discovery that hunters and gatherers tend to have greater drunkenness than groups with herding or agricultural economies. However, Field attributed this phenomenon to the social organization characteristic of hunting tribes rather than to fears about adequate subsistence. Field found that insobriety was positively associated with informal, friendly, personal interaction, such as that often found in egalitarian societies, and that sobriety was associated with formal, hierarchical social structure. Degree of drunkenness also was found to be tied to bilateral descent and bilocal or neolocal postmarital residence. Relative sobriety was to be found in those societies having corporate unilineal descent groups, particularly patrilineal ones, and patrilocal and perhaps avunculocal postmarital residence. The general idea that emerges from Field's analysis is that drunken tribes have great freedom of personal choice and expression, bilateral descent, and an egalitarian, nonhierarchical sociopolitical system. Sober tribes, by contrast, put greater restraints on personal choice and expression, usually have corporate unilineal kin groups, and an authoritarian, hierarchical sociopolitical system in which power to punish wrongdoers resides in the hands of political leaders.

At first glance, Field's theory appears to offer a good explanation of the nature of drinking and drunkenness in Greater Trukese Society. Truk is fundamentally egalitarian and nonhierarchical in its traditional socio-political makeup. Despite this, personal choice and expression are not given completely free rein, and individuals frequently are forced to conform to the wishes of their kinsmen, especially their senior kinsmen. Trukese social organization consists of corporate matrilineages grouped into named exogamous clans, but the power of lineage leaders to impose their wishes on others or to punish transgressions has always been quite severely limited (see, e.g., Swartz 1959). Field puts considerable weight on the clan-community, arguing that "our data show that as the community approaches an exogamous clan organization, drunkenness decreases" (1962:61). But once more the Trukese situation fails to support his theory: communities in Greater Trukese Society are organized into exogamous unilineal clans, but the rate of drunkenness is high. On balance, Truk appears to possess a mix of features that Field associates either with drunken tribes or with sober tribes, but not with both.

There is unanimity among writers on Trukese sociopolitical organization that the traditional system was quite limited in scope and structural intricacy. For example, Murdock and Goodenough (1947:334) state that the "political structure in Micronesia is in general characterized by a striking degree of complexity. Truk and the surrounding coral atolls [Greater Trukese Society] constitute the outstanding exception." Clifton maintains that Trukese political units "were little more than local communities within which individuals tended to intermarry, and because of their loose structuring and the absence of larger political aggregations or stable confederations, we must describe Trukese political structure as atomistic and stateless" (1964:95). Although some scholars might wish to argue that contemporary Truk has a very "tight" social system, clearly in comparison with other Micronesian societies Truk is loosely organized. Truk's combination of corporate unilineal descent and egalitarian non-hierarchical politics means that Field's theory would predict moderate to strong, but certainly not extreme, drunken behavior. Yet those who have compared alcohol use in different Micronesian societies (e.g., Mahoney 1974) have placed Truk at the most extreme end of a scale of disruptive drinking (cf. discussion on dependency below). We noted above, in discussing Horton's anxiety theory, that Yap and Palau have been pointed out as other Micronesian cultures characterized by a high degree of anti-social drunkenness, approaching, if not surpassing, Greater Trukese Society. In keeping with Field's theory, Yap and Palau should have bilateral descent and egalitarian sociopolitical systems. But precisely the opposite is the case. Not only do both societies have unilineal descent, but their hierarchical nature has led some to refer to them as caste systems. Field's hope that social organizational differences would provide the answer for observed cross-cultural differences in the incidence and style of drinking is therefore not met by Truk and other Micronesian societies.

DEPENDENCY

A few years after Field published his reinterpretation of Horton's findings, Bacon, Barry, and Child (henceforth BBC) (1965) summarily rejected both of these earlier theories and offered a new approach to the problem. They argued that patterns of drinking relate primarily to anxiety and conflict over dependency needs and set out to examine the hypothesis that "amounts and patterns of alcohol consumption by adults have their antecedents partly in the degree and pattern of nurturance in infancy, the extent of demands for self-reliance and achievement in childhood, and the extent to which the expression of dependent needs is permitted in adult life" (1965:31). They anticipated that the degree of drinking, drunkenness, or both would be positively correlated with demands for self-reliance and achievement in childhood and negatively correlated with the indulgence of dependency needs in infancy, childhood, and adulthood.

By the time BBC began their research, better cross-cultural samples than that used by Horton and Field were at hand. Accordingly, their sample consisted of 139 societies from all over the world (except Europe). One society in their sample was Truk.

BBC first had to code each society according to a set of variables useful for their purposes. To the limit that information existed, every society in their sample was coded for such factors as general aspects of drinking (e.g., availability, extent, frequency, quantity); contexts of drinking by frequency and quantity (e.g., religious, ceremonial, household, party); behavior associated with drinking by intensity, degree of change from sober behavior, and the extremity of the behavior (e.g., sociability, exhibitionism, hostility, rule breaking); and other extreme behavior (e.g., passing out, vomiting, guilt). Each society also was coded for such items as nurturance, approval of drinking, and approval of drunkenness. It is a commentary on the frequent shallowness of cross-cultural studies of this sort that of the twenty-two Pacific Island cultures[6] in the BBC sample, only three cases are useful.[7] Only for the Ifaluk, Maori, and Ulithians are BBC able to code more than 10 percent of the possible items. Even in the best of these cases, only about one third of the potential items actually had data available for coding. Once again we see that our understanding of drinking by Pacific Islanders is woefully deficient.

Another problem with cross-cultural samples of the sort employed by BBC is that interpretations and conclusions are only as good as the original ethnographic data. In the case of Oceania, as we have just seen, the quality of BBC's data is not very impressive. Beyond this, however, BBC erroneously report that the Carolinians[8] and the people of Ifaluk Atoll had alcoholic beverages aboriginally (see Marshall and Marshall 1975), and they indicate that there are no sex differences in alcohol use among either Carolinians or Samoans (for contradictory evidence see Lemert

1964; Marshall and Marshall 1975). Finally, several groups that BBC treat as separate cultures in their sample are so closely related to each other that they probably do not merit division into "unique cultures" (e.g., Carolinians/Ifaluk/Ulithians and Lau Fijians/Vanua Levu).[9]

Bacon, Barry, Child and Snyder (1965) were able to code only nine of the ninety-seven possible items in their comparative tables for Truk: type of beverage; use of alcohol aboriginally and postcontact; sex differences in use of alcohol; extent of ritualization (males only); frequency of drinking as religious ritual (males only); frequency of public or ceremonial drinking (males only); intensity of hostility (males only); extent of change in hostility (males only); and occurrence of extreme hostility (males only). For our purposes, their most interesting findings on Trukese drinking have to do with hostility and its expression.

Three measures of hostility were coded. No society in the BBC sample was rated higher than Truk on the "intensity of hostility" measure. Only four other societies were rated equally high out of fifty-three cases where a rating could be made, putting Truk in the upper 9 percent of codable societies on the intensity of drunken hostility. When "extent of change in hostility" is considered, Truk does not occupy so dramatically high a position when compared with other societies in the BBC sample. Of the fifty-two societies coded on this item, sixteen ranked higher than Truk and ten others ranked as high. The "occurrence of extreme hostility" measure restores Truk to near the top of the list in terms of drunken aggression. Only two of the sixty-two societies coded on this item ranked higher and eight others were rated as high, placing Truk in the upper 18 percent of the codable sample.

Whatever the faults of BBC's cross-cultural coding, we may legitimately conclude from their tables that when weekend warfare is compared with drunken comportment in a multitude of other societies, it shows up as quite violent behavior. Physical combat involving injury is likely to occur with substantial frequency, and fearsome Trukese drunks undergo a fairly striking change in demeanor from their sober state. All of this confirms what we have found in earlier chapters, but now we have the advantage of a wider cross-societal perspective from which to view this behavior.

Dependency theory initially seems to hold the key for helping us understand Trukese drunken comportment since those who have probed the Trukese psyche tell us that unfulfilled dependency needs account in large measure for the personalities typical of Trukese adults (e.g., Gladwin and Sarason 1953). After analyzing their data, BBC found that "indulgence of dependence is negatively related to frequency of drinking" and that "societies which indulge dependency needs in infancy and childhood tend to show less alcohol consumption than those which are less indulgent" (1965:35).

For the first year or two of life most dependency needs are satisfied instantly for a Trukese infant. Babies are given the breast or bottle whenever they cry. They are continually held and fondled by loving adults and older children, and it seems that the world is at their beck and call. With all this attention, however, infant feeding is inconsistent: a mother may nurse her child only briefly when it cries, become interested in someone else or something else, and put the child down again before it is satiated. On account of these short, interrupted feeding periods, Fischer believes that "Trukese babies meet with important frustrations in attempting to satisfy their oral needs" (1950:82). Fischer suggests that

> The short feeding periods of the infant may be responsible for the development in the adult personality and in the social system of extreme emphasis on food, in a land of relative plenty. On the other hand, the great emphasis on food in the social system and the great desire on the part of the individual to be made happy by being filled up with it, no doubt leads to the verbally expressed theory of child feeding, to give the baby all it wants to eat, when it wants it. [1950:83]

Even allowing for these relatively minor frustrations of dependency in infancy, matters change abruptly and radically when the young Trukese child is weaned. The experience is made even more traumatic if a new sibling has supplanted him at his mother's breast. The screams of young children, which formerly brought attention and gratification, now are ignored or even punished. The warm nurturant environment of infancy is suddenly replaced by an uncertain environment dominated by inconsistency of response on the part of adults and older children. A young child is never sure whether his behavior or misbehavior will be overlooked or whether he will be struck or verbally reprimanded for his actions.[10] As the child grows older, "he is gradually forced into a position of taking responsibility for the needs of others by suffering worse pain if he does not relinquish his own desires so that those of others may be satisfied. ...*This appears to be more true for female than for male children*" (Fischer 1950:87; emphasis added). The one theme running through all this is inconsistency of response. Greater Trukese Society is a classic case of a social system that both indulges and frustrates the expression of dependency needs by infants and young children. Following BBC's theory, we would expect to find fairly heavy drinking on the part of all Trukese adults.[11] But this is not what we discover at all: at least one half of all adults—the women—undergo the same early childhood socialization with its attendant frustrations, but most of them rigidly eschew alcohol.

Dependency theory also predicts that heavy demands for self-reliance and achievement in childhood will be positively associated with amounts and patterns of alcohol consumption. But once again the Trukese data do not entirely conform to expectations. It is the case that young men in late adolescence and in their twenties must forcefully establish personal reputations for self-reliance and achievement. But neither in the definition BBC appear to use nor in the Trukese view are these young men "children." Unless we alter the age category about which we are speaking from "childhood" to "young adulthood," this aspect of dependency theory does not seem to fit the Trukese data. For it is precisely at the point in life when Trukese males must prove themselves competent and adequate persons that alcohol consumption and crazy drunken comportment both rise dramatically.

The final part of BBC's dependency theory is well supported by the Trukese data. They predict that the degree of drinking, drunkenness, or both will be negatively correlated with the permission of dependent behavior on the part of adults. In chapter 5, it was documented at some length that Trukese males are expected to display a macho exterior and to hold most of their emotions under rather tight rein. Among the emotions considered inappropriate for a real man to display are those showing dependency and weakness: open weeping and an inability to take care of oneself physically, for example. These "dependent" emotions are associated with femininity in the Trukese view. Thus adult males from their late teens on find it difficult to openly express dependency except when they are drunk. Women, on the other hand, may openly display these emotions. As BBC predict, men drink while women do not.

Dependency theory, then, is partially supported and partially refuted by the Trukese data, depending on the stage of life focused on. We turn now to the fourth and final major theory.

POWER

The fourth theory that seeks to explain drinking differences in cross-cultural perspective is known as the "power theory." Although McClelland and his associates (1966) originally proposed the power theory on the basis of an analysis of folk tale content, they have subsequently expanded their studies to include a number of experimental and ethnographic contributions (McClelland et al. 1972). The gist of the power theory is that people drink alcoholic beverages to attain feelings of personal strength and power and that high levels of drinking will be found in those cultures where average individual concerns about power are high.

As with the other major theories we have examined, the power theory has a certain attractiveness as an explanation for why Trukese drink. We have seen that young men are very much concerned with establishing themselves as powerful persons characterized by courage and strong thought, and this would seem to be precisely in line with the assumptions of McClelland and his coworkers. Before we jump to any hasty conclusions, however, we should look into this explanation more carefully.

Much of the aggression that comes out in Trukese drunkenness is not directed at building a public reputation for manliness. Rather it is an opportunity to strike back at someone without the likelihood of direct or immediate reprisal. Many Trukese young men drink for recognition and to force others to notice and take account of them (cf. Mohatt 1972:269). Thus, while the power theory may partially explain the fighting among young men themselves, it does not adequately explain male aggression against females, the aggression of drunks against their sober siblings, or the suicides that occur when Trukese young men have been drinking (see chapter 4). Being drunk gives a young man unusual control over others because it allows him to act and communicate *his* definition of relationships while being culturally viewed as irresponsible. Trukese drunks are able to send to others what Gorad et al. (1971:653–54) call "multiple incongruent messages," which enable them to be in an advantageous and powerful position over those with whom they interact.

Quite often young men get drunk to express aggression against members of the older generation. There is a tension between senior and junior generations in Truk that always lies simmering just below the surface. This tension is a result of one's lifelong dependency on others in one's lineage or family group for one's welfare and the fact that lineage authority is based strictly on age seniority. As Goodenough notes, "for most of his life every individual is subject to someone else's power to veto most of his major decisions. . . . No Trukese can revolt against this authority because he has no place to go if he does" (1966:223). Although I would not state the matter quite so strongly (there are, for example, other places for a Trukese to go via avenues of created kinship), I believe Goodenough's emphasis on latent intergenerational hostilities is correctly placed. Not only are young men in a most stressful psychological position in Trukese culture, but they must also endure the frustration of being viewed as unimportant. Their opinions are seldom sought, and they are rarely invited to attend, much less speak out at, meetings where important decisions are to be made. This traditional powerlessness of the younger generation vis-à-vis the older is widespread in Micronesia. Liquor has allowed the open expression of intergenerational antagonisms in at least one community in Greater Trukese Society in recent years (Marshall 1975a). Although it is possible to interpret drinking by young men as a search for personal power, I think such an interpretation misses the point. The drunkenness of young men does not bring them any power over the older generation, but it does permit them to vent hostility against their seniors whom they are loath to attack directly even when inebriated. It is true in some cases, however, that drunken defiance of the older generation by young men may lead ultimately to a shift in the balance of power between the generations in the arena of introduced, elective municipal politics, as distinct from that of lineage affairs (Marshall 1975a). Like the other theories we have reviewed, then, this one provides a partial but not a final explanation for the complex dynamics of drunken comportment in Truk.

ASSESSING THE ALTERNATIVES

We have had a look at distilled versions of four major theories for observed cross-cultural differences in drinking and drunken comportment and we have found each of these wanting as a completely adequate explanation for drunkenness in Greater Trukese Society. A major reason why each of these theories fails is that the proponents of each put forth their explanation as the only adequate one, more or less exclusive of others. If anthropologists have learned one thing over the years, however, it is that simple, monocausal explanations for the complex, multivariate phenomena of human social behavior in discrete cultural settings are hopelessly misguided. Might it be the case that all four theories we have reviewed contain a germ of truth concerning why Trukese drink as they do? This issue is examined in chapter 8. For the moment we can briefly summarize the major features of these four theories that may help us understand weekend warfare in Truk.

Trukese do have a great many anxieties associated with food-getting activities and eating, and particularly younger Trukese in the district center are exposed to a host of new acculturative pressures that did not impinge on previous generations. It seems plausible that such anxieties may play some role in the drunkenness of young men. The fragmentation and nonhierarchical nature of traditional Trukese political organization was shown to conform with some of Field's findings about the extent and frequency of drunkenness, even though his social organization theory ran aground on the shoal of corporate unilineal descent groups in Truk. Still, the fact that Trukese drinking appears to be the most extreme in the Trust Territory, coupled with the fact that Truk's sociopolitical organization is atypical of Micronesian societies, gives one pause before rejecting out of hand a possible association between these two findings. Third, the capricious nature of child rearing in Truk and other aspects of dependency theory seem to fit reasonably well with the Trukese case, even if dependency fails to account for the sexual differences that exist in alcohol use in Truk. Finally, given the core Trukese values of bravery and strong thought, both of which put a premium on personal power and manliness, one is reluctant to dismiss utterly the power theory as at least one part of an equation that may solve the problem of why Trukese get drunk in so rowdy a manner.

111

Running Amok in Truk

7

With the disappearance of warfare, the handling of
aggression becomes an anxiety-provoking problem.
. . . Indeed, in a tribe with a warrior tradition and a
positive value placed on assertiveness and aggression,
the state of drunkenness may be approved precisely
because it facilitates the conduct that the society
basically values.

> J. Levy and S. J. Kunitz, Indian
> Drinking: Navajo Practices and
> Anglo-American Theories

One of the most crucial problems which faces the
Trukese is that of the expression of aggression.

> T. Gladwin and S. B. Sarason, Truk:
> Man in Paradise

THE TRUCULENT TRUKESE DRUNK

Drunkenness in Truk closely resembles the special type of insanity among
the inhabitants of the D'Entrecasteaux Islands that is characterized by a
murderous frenzy and called "amok" by Chowning (1961) and Fortune
(1963). Amok behavior in the D'Entrecasteaux Islands, like wild man behavior in New Guinea, gives an individual license to aggress against
others without penalty. Those who run amok in Truk are always drunk
on alcohol. Although not every drunk in Truk becomes a sardine, it is important to emphasize that every drunk may take on this identity. In this

chapter we explore the Trukese version of temporary insanity brought on by consumption of alcohol by looking at how the identity of the drunk is learned, under what circumstances it is adopted, and how the concepts of *time out* and *within-limits* developed by MacAndrew and Edgerton (1969) apply to the truculent Trukese drunk.

THE DRAMA OF DRINKING

A number of different writers have shown how out-of-the-ordinary behaviors like temporary madness and drunkenness may be interpreted as dramatic performances in which individuals may manipulate the public image of themselves (see, e.g., Clarke 1973; Dennis 1975; Newman 1964; Robbins 1973). A similar approach to Trukese drunkenness is taken in this section.

Trukese recognize that most young men who drink and subsequently engage in weekend warfare do so to impress others—particularly the young ladies—with their bravery, strength, and willingness to fight and take risks. Many Trukese also explicitly recognize that those who "run amok" are not really as out of control as they might appear to an outsider unversed in the rules of the game.

Everyone knows in Truk that drunks are dangerous, crazy, just like animals, and beyond reason because they cannot "hear" anything that is said to them. Everyone in Truk also agrees that drunks may get away with things that sober persons may not: they may disturb the peace, openly court women, brawl with each other, destroy property, attack sober persons (including close kinsmen), and occasionally even kill someone. They are not held responsible for what they say or do because, after all, they are crazy and do not know what they are doing. Everyone in Truk also knows that the above sketch of drunkenness is a shared fiction. Drunks are not truly insane, they are only held to be so temporarily at particular times, in particular places, and in regard to specific persons. Like New Guinea wild men and those who run amok in the D'Entrecasteaux Islands, Trukese drunks can and do discriminate contexts and persons, and they guide their crazy behavior accordingly.

In chapter 4, case 1, I pointed out that X, whom everyone agreed was crazy at the time, assiduously avoided throwing rocks at my house during his drunken rampage, even though he flung rocks in every other direction. I also noted that X's demeanor almost completely reversed itself a short while later when he came to pay me a visit. In chapter 4, case 7, D, who was running amok and attacking everyone in sight, suddenly drew up short when he observed me watching him and walked over almost amicably, trying to explain his actions to me in apologetic English. Following our brief interchange, D continued to run amok. If these two men were crazy and out of control, why was I not attacked like the rest? I contend

113

that I was treated differently because these men were quite aware of what they were doing and that a great deal of their craziness was put on like an actor's mask.[1]

Informants from Peniyesene repeatedly assured me that a man with a grudge against another will always get drunk before seeking out the subject of his ire. Once recognized as drunk, he will come spoiling for a showdown, quite capable of discriminating the individual he is seeking from others with whom he may come in contact. Getting drunk, that is, putting on the mask of temporary insanity, is considered a necessary excuse by everyone; once drunk, the grudge-bearer can openly express his hostility without culpability for his outburst. The belief that alcohol can be used as a "cover" for otherwise unforgivable behavior also was recorded by Mahoney:

> One Trukese informant offered an example: "Suppose I want to take revenge? First I will get drunk. Then I can beat up the man on whom I want revenge. Nobody will say very much because I'm drunk" [1974:53]

As I have argued elsewhere (Marshall 1975a), it seems clear that much drunkenness in Greater Trukese Society is feigned in the sense that drunks are not physiologically inebriated and are usually quite aware and in control of their actions.[2] Viewed from this perspective it becomes useful to analyze the rampaging of truculent Trukese drunks as an ongoing series of dramatic performances.

In preceding chapters we have noted that drunken brawls, replete with the showmanship of kung fu, provide important public spectacles in which reputations are made and modified on the basis of the adequacy of one's performance. Drunken carousing also has been pointed to as the major means for young men to "strut their stuff" before members of the opposite sex, perhaps substituting in large measure for traditional dancing. Drunkenness has also been cited as a major way for gaining public attention while airing a grievance and ridding oneself of pent-up aggressive feelings. In all of these cases the crucial ingredient is the public nature of the performance before a community audience. All these actions would be meaningless were they performed alone without riveting the attention of the community.

The literature on New Guinea wild men again bears scrutiny for the useful insights it offers on why drunks run amok in Truk. In Truk, as in New Guinea, it is not pure happenstance that those most likely to become temporarily mad are young men:

> Young men in traditional times when oppressed or confused by the demands of cultural order could temporarily free themselves through madness, a diversion that may have made it easier to

pass into a new stage of life. Today, a modified form of madness offers a similar escape from new demands and confusions. [Clarke 1973:211]

While they are mad, these young men, both in Truk and in New Guinea, gain community attention and fulfill for a time "the cultural ideal of being an aggressive and dramatic man" (Clarke 1973:208). Along these same lines Newman argues that interpretations of wild man behavior

> must take into account the community within which the individual displays the behavior, the effect this display may have on community opinion of the person, and the ideological background against which the behavior is played out. These are important factors, for in addition to providing an outlet for aggressive impulses, such behavior also serves as a means whereby the individual can forcefully and dramatically cause the community to revise its image of him. . . . Such a pattern can thus be viewed as instrumental behavior redefining the social situation of the person displaying it and depending for its success on community acceptance of the portrayal [1964:1]

Contemporary drunken behavior by Trukese young men is an exact cultural analogue of wild man behavior in New Guinea; it represents a different, alternative solution to the same kind of problem. Crazy drunken behavior in Truk occurs only among young adult males of a restricted age group—the exact same group where wild man behavior is found among the Gururumba. And in Truk, as in the latter cultural setting, "it can be shown that men in this category are subject to unique kinds of social pressures and that wild man behavior is understandable as a response to these pressures" (Newman 1964:9). The one description I have read of women becoming mad in New Guinea (Frankel 1976) simply serves to reinforce the notion that this role is a positively sanctioned one that permits individuals to work out stresses brought about by commonly recurring social pressures.[3] Frankel indicates that many of the young women of Telefomin who became mad were in the throes of painful disagreements with close kin. He states that "there are reasons for considering that the position of young women in Telefomin is particularly stressful" (1976:121).

LEARNING TO BE A DRUNK

What people do after they have consumed alcoholic beverages has been rather conclusively shown to be largely a matter of what their culture teaches them they can and cannot do (see MacAndrew and Edgerton 1969 for numerous well-documented examples of this). If we accept this view

115

that drunken comportment is primarily learned behavior, then we must reject the conventional wisdom that alcohol is a solvent of the superego that causes a loosening of the inhibitions, leading people to behave in socially unacceptable ways. How do young Trukese males learn to behave as proper drunks?

While different vogues have come and gone in learning theory, one idea has remained constant through the years: imitation of adults by children is a fundamental aspect of the learning process. Clearly, in American culture, our children will normally seek to emulate what we do. Trukese children are no different.

The most exciting and colorful daily events in Peniyesene are the drunken antics of young men. These events inevitably attract a horde of small children who hang around the perimeter of the audience. From early childhood on, Trukese children carefully and frequently observe drunken performances. By the time boys reach age 8 or 10, they begin to imitate the swaggering style of young men.[4]

Boys approaching their teens become attentive to the finest details of young male drunken comportment. Kung fu routines are practiced diligently, war cries are tried out, and special gaits characteristic of drunks are affected. But imitative learning does not stop here. Boys 8 to 10 years old will ferret empty booze bottles out of the thickets to sniff them and get high. Having done so, they will stagger about with bottle in hand, occasionally uttering the Trukese war cry and falling down as drunks do. The difference is that when the boys collapse they collapse in giggles.

Despite such practice, youngsters of either sex up to age 14 or 15 seem at least mildly afraid of drunks and will run away rapidly at their approach. Actually, running from the drunk is treated more like a game by older children; only the very young children are truly frightened. Regarding the myth that Trukese drinkers are out of control, not once did I observe or hear of a drunk striking a child in spite of endless opportunities for them to do so.

Another point that underscores the dramaturgical quality of drinking behavior by Trukese young men is the striking shift in comportment when they reach manhood. It is thought shameful for an adult man to act like a young man after he has consumed alcohol, and he is openly mocked by his peers if he continues to do so. Just as boys learn drunken comportment appropriate to the young adult status they will enter, so young men must learn the style of drunken comportment befitting an adult male member of the community. The same beverages are consumed by the same persons in approximately the same amounts at different times in their lives. The superegos of these men do not change. Their inhibitions do not tighten up with advancing years. What has changed is the set of public expectations surrounding appropriate behavior for men at different stations in life.

A final example that illustrates the dramatic aspect of drunken behavior in Truk should be mentioned. When Trukese young men are placed in radically different social settings away from Truk, they often alter the script for rowdy drunken comportment accordingly.[5] I have personally seen Trukese young men drink in the homes of Americans in the United States and maintain their composure throughout the evening despite taking in a considerable amount of ethanol. Similarly, Mahoney (1974:35) comments on what he calls "new elite drinkers" in the Trust Territory "who are able to drink heavily for long periods, yet remain in control of their physical and mental functioning." These are both clear examples of what MacAndrew and Edgerton (1969) call "the sway of time and circumstance."

Appearing drunk in order to assume the social identity of the drunk is not a situation limited only to Greater Trukese Society. For example, the same sort of situation has been described for a Mexican village where "it becomes apparent that social drunkenness really defines the drunk's role, and not physiological inebriation. Amilpas drunks are often suspected of not really being as drunk as they seem, in order to perform otherwise unacceptable acts with impunity" (Dennis 1975:862). To don the "drunk" identity and legitimately express one's hostile feelings, a Trukese must broadcast the message that he is drunk. Typical cues are loud, boisterous speech, war cries, unsteady gait, the smell of alcohol, and a bottle or beer can in hand. Having thus advertised his social identity and "once identified and defined by everyone present as drunk, the individual may then proceed to send other messages all of which will be qualified by 'I am drunk' and that one should not hold him responsible for what he does or says" (Gorad et al. 1971:653).

If physical inebriation does not always accompany the social identity of the drunk in Greater Trukese Society, this raises the question, How often are drunks literally out of control of their physical and mental functioning? Most of the time young men who imbibe alcohol in Truk are able to maintain a degree of control over themselves even though in outward appearance they may look crazy. Because they are held to be temporarily mad, the controls under which they must operate are less stringent than those which apply to sober persons. Phrased differently, when Trukese drunks go crazy, they only go so crazy, and they only go crazy in culturally approved ways.

This view of the problem follows very closely the work of MacAndrew and Garfinkel (1962) and MacAndrew and Edgerton (1969). Rejecting the "conventional scientific wisdom" which explains the enabling role of alcohol on the basis of its toxic assault on the "higher centers of the brain," they advocate "changing our interpretive focus from the 'level' of the organism to that of the social system. . . . Such an approach would ignore the physiological consequences of alcohol ingestion and would focus instead upon the meanings accorded the resultant state of intoxication by the members of the system" (MacAndrew and Garfinkel 1962:263). Although I do not believe we can entirely ignore the physiological consequences of alcohol ingestion, I think these men have pointed out a useful direction for those of us seeking to understand drunken comportment, as opposed to those scholars who pursue the rosetta stone that will explain at one stroke the complex psychophysiological affliction of alcoholism.

Putting on the mantle of drunkenness in Truk allows a man to engage in a wide range of normally prohibited behaviors without censure. Some, if not all, of these behaviors involve complex processes of impression management. Thus, to be thoroughly intoxicated and out of control would likely prove self-defeating. For instance, a young man so plastered that he could be easily beaten by an adversary in a fight would lose prestige along with the fight. A young man so drunk that he could not successfully approach potential lovers to "hustle" them would find his love life bleak indeed. It is important in Truk to have consumed some alcohol in order to assume the identity of the drunk, but it is also important not to have consumed too much. Those who fail to learn this turn out to be losers.

THE MESSAGE IN THE MADNESS

We have seen that alcohol use enables young men to build public reputations in keeping with basic Trukese values and that it facilitates the acquisition of sweethearts for a young man by allowing him to display his wares and to approach young women in public without fear of gossip. We have also seen that alcohol use puts in abeyance a number of injunctions governing proper kinship behavior among sober persons. But what lies at the heart of all this? Does alcohol only serve a number of social functions as a surrogate for traditional behaviors like warfare and dancing that have now disappeared? What is the message in the madness that is weekend warfare in Truk?

I believe the answer to these questions lies readily at hand when we turn to the matter of aggression and its control and expression in Greater Trukese Society. Trukese drunks who become sardines do not do so "just for kicks." There is always a method in their madness:

> The men who became sardines at a yeast drinking party [on Etal Atoll] were invariably known to be in the midst of some wrenching interpersonal dispute with another islander, usually a kinsman. . . . In other words, a sardine could express his anger and frustration publicly (and in the process force or attempt to force the issue to some resolution) . . . in a context of rather sympathetic public regard. He was excused on the basis that he was drunk and

therefore temporarily "out of his mind," and thus he did not realize the seriousness of this breach of common proper behavior. [Nason 1975:623–24]

A young man becomes a sardine only when caught up in some trying personal difficulty—for example, an argument with a friend or relative, rejection by a sweetheart, or public derision for his lack of manliness. The message in the madness of Trukese drunkenness is that in assuming the social identity of the drunk, in putting on the culturally approved mask of temporary insanity, one may legitimately express aggression against others and be excused for doing so. When we learn that previous research indicates Truk to be a culture in which outlets for aggression are not readily available, this explanation becomes even more compelling.

Some of the public display aspects of drunken behavior occur when sober persons lose their tempers as well. Issuing the Trukese war cry is a means for arresting public attention whether drunk or sober. Heaving rocks at the house of a person who has raised one's ire is a common way for publicly demonstrating extreme displeasure. Destroying personal property is another means employed by drunk and sober persons alike to vent anger.[6] Threatening or actually committing suicide as a means of revenge against close kin is a behavior that has existed in Trukese culture since long before alcoholic beverages were introduced. In illustration of some of this, consider the following extract from John Westwood's memoirs of Lukunor in 1878:

> They are quickly angered, but their usual practice at such times is to go and hew down their own trees or destroy anything belonging to themselves, yelping all the time as though they were really bereft of their senses until their friends intervene. Sometimes they will go so far as to rush into the bush and hang themselves, or sent [sic] out to sea in fragile canoes never to return. [1905:109]

Compare this with Nason's description of typical sardine behavior ninety years later on the neighboring atoll of Etal: "A sardine would wrestle with his companions, lose his temper and attempt to fight others, pound on houses, throw rocks or sticks aimlessly or at others or at houses, and cry or shout until he was subdued or stopped of his own accord" (1975:620–21). Finally, recall the details of the case studies from Peniyesene presented in chapter 4, wherein rushing about, shouting, wrestling, throwing rocks, and occasional suicide are all prominently displayed. It appears that the nature of expressing aggression in Greater Trukese Society has not changed much over the years since alcoholic beverages were introduced. The state of drunkenness simply opened up new possibilities for the open expression of antisocial impulses. In this sense, drunkenness may be looked upon as a psychological blessing for young men in Truk from the standpoint of their overall mental health. Rather than bottling up much of their aggression, they could now freely express it in a socially sanctioned way. As MacAndrew and Garfinkel put it, "It is not that 'When I am drunk, it *happens* to me that I become assertive', but rather, 'Being drunk *allows* me to be assertive'" (1962:264).

We are fortunate that Truk is a culture that has received considerable attention from psychological anthropologists. It is of no small consequence for the argument being developed here that all of these scholars find aggression management to be a major serious problem for the Trukese. Over and over again, Gladwin and Sarason (1953:227–28) drive this point home. Another psychologically oriented anthropologist who carried out research in Truk argues that "the expression and inhibition of aggression is the central conflict in the personalities of most Trukese" and that "the Trukese are virtually never free from aggressive feelings that seek expression" (Swartz 1965:32, 38). Getting drunk solves these problems at one swallow for young men in Truk.

The reasons Trukese took to alcoholic beverages with such alacrity and the reasons for the belligerent fashion of drunken comportment by Trukese young men now begin to fall into place. Like every culture, Trukese culture has certain internal contradictions that set up stress points for persons occupying particular social positions. One such contradiction is the emphasis on bravery as a core value balanced off against respectfulness. Keeping one's public performance in accord with these two somewhat opposed values presents young men, especially, with a difficult task at which many do not succeed. Another major contradiction in Trukese culture has to do with the expectations males, in particular, must meet to be considered ideal persons. The difficulty of proving oneself a man of bravery, respectfulness, strong thought, learnedness, and *machismo* is great, and many Trukese young men find themselves unable to live up to these standards. In nearly every way, young men are under severe social and psychological pressure to prove themselves worthy of public respect and attention by adequate, competent performance in a variety of test situations. Young men must meet and master a plethora of risks. Young men must win in the competitive contests they engage in with their sweethearts. Young men must succeed in the introduced system of formal education and wage employment to be considered learned. The physical, intellectual, productive, and sexual capabilities of young men are on trial. And some young men emerge from the fray as losers, with public reputations as "no-counts" and with bruised and battered self-images.

Enter alcoholic beverages, which provided a perfect solution to the problem of how to express aggression legitimately. Alcohol not only facilitated the achievement of the cultural ideal of masculinity, but its pharmacologic properties salved the damaged egos of those who fell short of the mark. The ideals of bravery and manly thought involved aggressive assertiveness which drinking liquor aided and abetted. Trukese learned this from observations of the rough and rude style of drinking provided by the traders and other foreigners who camped among them in the 1890s and early 1900s (cf. Marshall and Marshall 1976). The macho image of Trukese males was strengthened by ethanol. The desire for vengeance that wells from deep within Trukese culture was well served by firewater. Those young men who failed the tests of competence, those who could not prove themselves real men, found relief in the sedation of physical and psychic pain that booze provided.

Perhaps it is not entirely fair to claim that the introduction of alcoholic beverages solved the problem of expressing aggression in Greater Trukese Society. It may be more accurate to state that drunkenness has provided a major new outlet for hostile feelings on the part of young men who seem always to have been in the most stress-ridden position in the social system. In this sense, weekend warfare is not a simple substitute for traditional warfare; rather it has allowed a rechanneling of aggressive impulses in more socially manageable ways.

This may help explain why the fearless Trukese warriors of the turn of the century put down their weapons so meekly in the face of the German edict to disarm and cease fighting. Introduced rifles and other firearms had enabled a dizzying spiral of interlineage and interdistrict warfare to get out of hand by 1904. Traditional warfare suddenly was no longer under any real social control—the vastly higher rate of death and injuries brought on with the new weapons gave the bitter feuding a new and frightening aspect to those engaged in it: the killing appeared to be escalating out of control without end. The German ultimatum allowed all sides to disengage without tarnishing their jealously guarded public reputations for bravery and strong thought. Perhaps of equal importance, drunkenness—which was just becoming popular in Truk—offered an attractive alternative.

Having learned how to drink and how to behave when drunk from watching the foreigners among them, Trukese young men employed the state of drunkenness to demonstrate their strength and manliness while greatly reducing the amount of killing in the process. The cultural demand for competent performance could still be met and the whole matter could again be controlled. But Trukese soon discovered that beverage alcohol offered an improvement on traditional means of expressing aggression and manliness. Not only could drunks confront their counterparts from other lineages or districts as they had in traditional warfare, but, again copying foreign models of comportment, they could also release aggressive impulses against close kin and friends without being held responsible. As long as they stayed within the bounds of the newly created script guiding proper drunken comportment, young men could vent their aggression without it getting out of hand. Also important was the development of the

121

idea that liquor freed a man's emotions from the rather heavy shackles under which they were normally kept, an idea probably taken from the example of the Japanese overlords. With this development, fearsome Trukese drunks tossed aside their stoic, macho exteriors and became maudlin sentimentalists who gave free rein to tears and other signs of "weakness." As drinking grew in popularity the condition of drunkenness came to be viewed as time out from everyday restrictions: when men fell under the influence of demon rum a new, more relaxed, set of limits went into effect.

In time out, everyone agrees that a person who is inebriated may operate with an altered state of conscience. He may say and do things not permitted those who have not declared time out, as long as the proper cues indicating the social identity he has assumed have been given. But just because time out is declared, rules governing social performance do not disappear altogether. Rather, a new set of rules is invoked which usually gives the inebriate much wider latitude of action but beyond which he must not transgress. This is what MacAndrew and Edgerton (1969) call the "within-limits clause."

Trukese drunkenness is time out from the normal social routine, but it is not without limits. It is guided by rather clear-cut rules governing who the actors may be, with whom they may interact, and how they should comport themselves. We have already seen that alcoholic beverages are associated with strength, power, and manliness. Those who lack strength, for example, small children and the elderly, should not consume spiritous liquors according to the Trukese script. It takes a strong person to manage strong drink. Nor should women imbibe, even though they have the necessary strength to do so according to my informants. For a woman to drink would violate the definition of femininity that has grown up in Truk, and it would compromise her public reputation as a good person. It would also rend the very fabric of Trukese society by threatening the viability of domestic life. The social actors in the drama of drinking, then, are limited to young men and adult men. While males in both these age categories may drink, Trukese expect adult men to put on a different play from that performed by young men.

Drunks are given carte blanche to approach anyone, but they may not attack just anyone. Children and the elderly are absolutely off limits. Although drunks may strike women, they do not actually do so very often. Drunks may chase women, say bad things to them, threaten and frighten them, but they may not beat them up with impunity. Any drunk who violates this proscription may expect swift retaliation from the woman's male kinsmen. Drunks may not physically attack their parents although they may verbally unburden themselves of their aggression, and can and do destroy property belonging to their parents.[7] The script guiding drunkenness allows for drunken young men to aggress against their siblings of

122

either sex—a behavior seldom permitted sober individuals—and siblings are the only persons who may properly intercept a drunk. Finally, although drunks may attack adult men, they rarely attack physically. Often they scream out their anger and frustration at an older male. Drunks may attack other young men, of course, and it is among drunken young men that the great majority of physical aggression rises to the surface.

FAILURE, STRESS, AND DRINKING

Historically, Truk has been a fundamentally egalitarian culture, and the value of strong thought involves a strong motivation not to be outdone by others. Recent developments throughout Micronesia, including Truk, have led to the growth of a social class hierarchy based primarily on material wealth and conspicuous consumption. Peniyesene, for example, consists rather strikingly of the "haves" and the "have nots." The gap between these two emergent classes appears to be rapidly widening. Moreover, the lack of meaningful economic development in Micronesia during the past thirty years has led to a sharp diminution in the number of wage jobs available to the ever larger number of young people who flood the job market each year. Thus, a great many young persons give up and drop out.

This response is common among many young men in Truk who see little or no future in continuing their education. Such a state of mind accounts for the fact that only one third of the young men between the ages of 15 and 24 from Peniyesene were in school during 1975–1976, and none was in high school. Their attitude is, "Why should I continue in school if after graduation no wage job will be available for me?" This attitude appears justified for Peniyesene young men, at least, when we recall that almost three quarters of the 15–29 age group is unemployed. Without succeeding in the formal educational system and unable to find paying jobs, young men in Peniyesene today are thwarted from proving themselves learned in the eyes of the community. They find it ever more difficult to "keep up with the Joneses." In frustration and despair some of these young men are turning to alcoholic beverages as a solace for failure and as a means of partially coping with this added life stress. Madsen (1974) has defined alcoholism as an affliction of persons who live in highly stressful psychological environments with which they cannot cope. Although I do not believe many—if any—Trukese young men are alcoholics by this or any other definition (see Postscript, p. 133), it will be important over the next few years to monitor the ways alcoholic beverages get used by the growing number of losers in the Trukese competition for masculine superiority.

Conclusions:
Alcohol, Aggression,
and the Trukese World View
8

It is useful to ask what the form and meanings of drink in a particular group tell us about their entire culture and society.

> D. Mandelbaum, "Alcohol and culture"

We shall attempt to explain drinking behavior as a consequence of cultural premises about reality. . . .

> W. Madsen and C. Madsen, "The cultural structure of Mexican drinking behavior"

EMOTION, COMMOTION, AND THE EXPRESSION OF AGGRESSION

Drunkenness among Trukese young men is fundamentally an emotional experience. This is particularly so after alcohol has been consumed, when young men become sardines and run amok through the villages. In this chapter I show how acts of drunkenness by young men in Truk satisfy their emotional needs in conformity with the emotional emphases of the culture as a whole. I indicate how this comes about by reference to the positive image of young men in Trukese culture as bacchanalian ne'er-do-wells (cf. Hamer 1965:298).

Whether drunk or sober, Trukese young men are looked upon as irresponsible. Traditionally and presently, they are not persons to be taken seriously in important community matters. Young men are expected to devote the bulk of their time and energies to the frivolous pursuits of drinking, courting sweethearts, and participating in singing groups that serenade young women by night with *itenipwin* 'love songs' (see Haser and White 1969 on this latter point). Quite literally, the life stage of the young male is seen as a time devoted to the pleasures of wine, women, and song, and not as a time of seriousness and purposefulness. Although young men are not expected to perform a great deal of productive work, they do contribute important labor on occasion by gathering breadfruit or coconuts, preparing pounded taro, going fishing, and, increasingly on Moen, bringing home a paycheck to be shared with their extended family.

A major part of the bacchanalian life-style of young men is given over to public displays of drunken bravado. These displays are a basic part of growing into manhood in Truk; they do not represent psychopathic or sociopathic behavior. They are expected and accepted parts of contemporary Trukese life, just as warfare and "heathen dancing" were regular parts of Trukese life a century ago.

We have seen that one hundred years of intensive outside contact have worked marked changes on many aspects of life in Truk, but that the set of beliefs Trukese hold about young men remains largely intact. Trukese young men continue to do as young men their age have always done in these islands. Public drunkenness is not a major new problem afflicting youth in Truk, rather it is merely the present-day mode of doing what young men have always done as they progress along the path to full-fledged manhood.

In chapter 7 the point was made that young men continue to be in what always has been the most stressful position in Trukese culture. These stresses derive from a host of factors, most of which have their genesis in traditional Trukese culture and social organization—for example, the combination of character traits believed to make up a good person, the emphasis on *machismo*, and the relative powerlessness of young men vis-á-vis their elders. Aboriginally, the major outlet through which young men could "blow off steam" generated by these social pressures was by waging warfare against other districts or islands. Quite fortuitously, as this outlet was closed off by German edict, a new outlet was offered in drunkenness. Trukese were quick to perceive the potential usefulness of drunkenness, and it soon became common behavior in the islands. Drinking and running amok in Truk therefore must be seen as a response by young men to stresses inherent in Trukese culture itself and not simply as a reaction to recent acculturative changes in the port town on Moen. Drunken craziness of the sort described in chapter 4 occurs throughout Greater Trukese Society and is not restricted to the port town where acculturative influences have had the greatest impact (see, e.g., Marshall 1975a; Nason 1975). In this respect, this study of Trukese drinking lends support and further confirmation to the position taken by Levy and Kunitz (1974) on Navajo drinking. They set out to investigate whether Indian drinking is best explained "by considering it as a retreatist or escapist response to social disintegration, or by viewing it as serving ends that are compatible with preexisting and persisting tribal institutions and values" (1974:3). They concluded that economic deprivation alone could not be used as an argument to explain the patterns of alcohol use they observed both on and off the Navajo Reservation. The same conclusion holds for the islands of Greater Trukese Society.

In chapter 7 we noted that a crucial problem facing Trukese is the expression of aggression. By the time the young men are socialized in their culture they have learned to hold their spontaneous feelings under tight passive control in keeping with the emphasis on *machismo*. Gladwin and Sarason suggest "that the Trukese outward passivity is a kind of learned defense against strong aggressive tendencies. . . . Not only do the Trukese have difficulty expressing strong or aggressive feeling but they appear to be in general a nonspontaneous people" (1953:227). Finally, these same authors note that "among the Trukese the display of aggression is the exception rather than the rule" (1953:228).

This tendency to suppress aggressiveness and other strongly felt emotions is quite similar to the situation Spiro describes for the nearby atoll of Ifaluk:

> This culture . . . is characterized by a strong sanction against aggression. No display of aggression is permitted in interpersonal relationships; and in fact, no aggression is displayed at all. The people could not remember one instance of anti-social behavior, *aside from the malebush*, nor were any examples of it observed in the course of this investigation. [1952:498; emphasis added]

On Ifaluk, as on Truk, people have difficulty directly expressing interpersonal aggression. Spiro argues that Ifaluk persons direct their antisocial impulses against malevolent ghosts as a socially acceptable channel for the expression of aggression and thus preserve harmony in the community. Persons who are *malebush* on Ifaluk are permitted to engage in antisocial behavior with only minimal interference from others (see, e.g., Spiro 1950). Spiro defines *malebush* as "all abnormalities—in which the Ifaluk include violations of the ethic of non-aggression, as well as what we would label mental subnormality, neurosis and psychosis" (1952:498). One who is *malebush* is believed to be possessed by a malevolent ghost. Such persons are not punished or chastised for violating the ethos of nonaggression because they are not deemed responsible for their behavior (Spiro 1953:92). This is precisely what we have found to be the case with

126

sardines in Greater Trukese Society. Sardines are temporarily insane and are therefore beyond the pale of normal social etiquette and responsibility. Malevolent ancestral spirits may possess a person on Ifaluk and allow him to express aggression without censure. Bottled, imported spirits may "possess" a person in Greater Trukese Society and allow him to violate the ethos of nonaggression that normally obtains in Trukese interpersonal relations.

Robbins discusses drunken episodes among the Naskapi Indians as "identity-resolving forums" in which drunks are permitted to defend a challenged identity, claim a desired identity, or rectify an identity that has been spoiled by failure. According to Robbins, "such interactions aim toward allowing the person to receive from others information which confirms the identity he is seeking" (1973:110). The drama of drinking by Trukese young men may be profitably looked at in the same way. In the commotion that accompanies drunkenness in Truk, young men simultaneously are able to work toward establishing the culturally valued identities of competence, true bravery, and manliness and to express aggression against others in socially permissible ways.

MEN AND WOMEN AGAIN

Nearly every major cross-cultural survey of drinking customs has found that males drink more frequently and heavily than females and that males express greater hostility than females when drunk. Even though men outdrink women in most of the world's cultures, very few cultures prohibit either sex access to alcohol. Child, Barry, and Bacon (1965) found that 96 percent of those societies for which adequate information existed (109/113) allowed both men and women to drink. Truk shows up as quite exceptional in this respect by not permitting women to drink,[1] and Greater Trukese Society also belies the major explanation put forth by Child, Barry, and Bacon to account for sex differences in drinking. These authors found that "alcohol was used aboriginally rather than being introduced postcontact in 81 percent of the societies with a definite sex difference but in only 45 percent of those without evidence of a sex difference. This difference has a very low probability of being due to chance . . ." (1965:56–57). While Child, Barry, and Bacon conclude that "it seems reasonable to expect that sex differences in drinking would be more likely to develop in societies which practiced it aboriginally," Trukese manifest a striking sex difference in alcohol use even though liquor was introduced postcontact.

I suggest that Truk's departure from the more typical pattern of alcohol use by both sexes can be explained by the basic cultural opposition between male and female (see chapter 5). Alcoholic beverages were rap-

127

idly incorporated into the male domain, and women were forbidden to consume them. But other differences between the sexes in Truk, as revealed by psychological anthropological research, help us to understand why drinking has remained exclusively a male preserve in Greater Trukese Society.

Gladwin and Sarason found major psychological differences between men and women in Truk. They maintain that "the nature of the differences and conflicts between adult men and women are of such a magnitude as to suggest that the origins of the differences should be found in the differential treatment of, attitudes toward, and expectations from boys and girls" (1953:236). It is exactly this combination—differential socialization for responsibility, cultural attitudes toward male and female, and cultural expectations of young men and young women—that we have used to account for the differences we observed in the way the sexes use or avoid alcoholic beverages. After assessing all the differences between the sexes in Truk, Gladwin and Sarason reach the conclusion that women are more secure and less anxious than men for a number of reasons. To begin with, women approach the sexual situation with less anxiety than men because the chances of their losing in the game of love are much less than for men. Moreover, "the control of food supplies provides the most crucial support for the pivotal position of the woman in the household and thus is the primary means whereby her social, and hence psychological, security is implemented in adulthood" (1953:245). Gladwin and Sarason also make much of the fact that men are less secure than women because males must leave their childhood home at puberty to avoid sleeping under the same roof as their sisters. Men also must reside away from their own close kin with members of their wives' lineages where they fall under the control of their wives' brothers (see, e.g., 1953:272–74). Finally, Gladwin and Sarason speculate that for Trukese the vagina rather than the penis is the primary symbol of sexuality and the role of a boy therefore is not looked upon as inherently superior in this culture.[2] The major point to be derived from Gladwin and Sarason's analysis of Trukese personality is that women in Truk are socially and psychologically more secure than men and this, in turn, helps us understand why young men are under greater psychological stress than young women in this culture.

A COMPOSITE EXPLANATION OF DRUNKENNESS IN TRUK

We return once more to the question of why young men in Truk get drunk in such an obstreperous fashion. There is no single, simple answer to this question. Drunkenness in Truk springs from multiple motives and satisfies a variety of needs, and there is considerable intracultural variation in drinking as in all else. Despite these caveats, I argue below that drunken craziness in Truk—whatever the motives that precipitate it in any individual—is made comprehensible to actor, audience, and outside observer alike by reference to certain basic premises in Trukese world view.

I have made much of the special stresses or anxieties that haunt young men in Truk, and I believe that Horton's theory that people drink liquor to reduce anxiety applies partially to the Trukese case. It must be emphasized, however, that the anxieties afflicting young men do not derive from subsistence worries or acculturative pressures alone, although the latter doubtless play a role in the drinking that occurs in the port town. The anxieties besetting males at the stage in life where they drink with greatest abandon have deep roots in Trukese culture and history.

The nature of Trukese social organization—particularly the stress on low-key, egalitarian leadership—has played a role in the evolution of Trukese drinking somewhat after the fashion suggested by Field. Although social organization taken by itself, does not come close to explaining the whole process, the absence of heavy-handed leaders who could quickly step in to enforce "law and order" and quell drunken disturbances certainly has facilitated the rise of the belligerent carousing so characteristic of Trukese boonie drinking today.

At several places in this book we have discussed the relative insecurity of Trukese men when compared to women. This insecurity leads to what Gladwin and Sarason call a "more acute" dependency on the part of men than of women (1953:288). Born of multiple inputs, this dependency appears to bedevil males throughout their lives; in combination with other "growing pains," it appears to reach a crescendo in young adulthood. Thus BBC's dependency theory definitely seems to play a part in any comprehensive explanation of why Trukese young men drink as they do.

Powerlessness is a special problem for young men in Greater Trukese Society. A lack of effective control over their own lives and a desire for a greater political voice than that traditionally accorded them may be increasing today. The winds of change sweeping over Micronesia carry a few successful young men to new heights never dreamed of, but these same winds simply bowl over many others, leaving them shaken and confused. The desire for greater personal and social power on the part of young Micronesian men (including but not limited to Trukese) comes out clearly in the results of a recent conference on Micronesia's youth held on Ponape. The young Micronesians attending this conference said that more than anything else they wanted to be appreciated and recognized by others; respected by others and possessed of self-respect; capable of making decisions and permitted by others to do so; responsible, independent, well educated, and productively employed (Hezel 1977:4) The adults at the conference wanted youth to be well educated yet willing to conform to a traditional life-style (including, presumably, traditional political arrangements); respectful toward their families and willing to contribute to the support of their relatives; church-goers, and restrained in the use of alcohol (Hezel 1977:4). Clearly, a discrepancy still exists between the power needs of youth and the attitudes toward these needs on the part of older persons in Micronesia. This discrepancy no doubt contributes to the style of drinking observed among young Trukese males.

Anxiety, social organization, dependency, and power contribute motives and arrangements that have influenced the evolution of Trukese drinking. None of these explanations, however, singly or collectively, suffices to explain the unique cast of Trukese drunken comportment. What does explain Trukese drunken comportment is culture—the peculiar system of symbols and meanings that persons sharing a common heritage learn, modify, and transmit through time to the next generation. Trukese culture provides an overarching framework within which anxiety, social organization, dependency, and power take on special meanings and are played out in specific ways according to shared understandings about the nature of reality.

I have argued that several major features of Trukese culture must be grasped before it is possible to understand drunken comportment in this society. These features include the basic system of values that combine to yield cultural images of good and bad persons. The positively valued personal attributes of bravery, respectfulness, and strong thought are achieved and validated in large part through drunken fighting, which has substituted for the major traditional avenue available for establishing a positive masculine image: warfare. Drunken fights just as importantly allow young men to avoid the despised labels of cowardice, arrogance, and weak thought; even in defeat a man can exhibit courage and strength. Another major feature of Trukese culture that must be understood before drunkenness by young men makes sense is the symbolism surrounding male and female. Alcohol and tobacco have been thoroughly incorporated into the exclusive male domain, so much so today that they have become primary symbols differentiating young men from young women. Young men are under tremendous pressure to use these substances; young women are under just as much pressure to avoid them. Finally, I have argued that the style of drunkenness in Truk does not completely become intelligible until one appreciates the difficulty Trukese always have had in handling aggression. To the extent that aggression has historically been a major problem in Trukese culture and personality, alcohol has been seized upon as a partial solution to this problem by allowing for periods of time out. Young men can aggress in socially sanctioned ways while they are looked upon as crazy and therefore not responsible for their words and deeds.

ETHOS AND ETHANOL

This book has to do most importantly with what Bateson called *ethos* in his classic study of the Iatmul culture of New Guinea. In part, Bateson drew his notion of ethos from the *Oxford English Dictionary* definition, which he gives as: "the characteristic spirit; prevalent tone of sentiment of a people or community; the 'genius' of an institution or system" (1958:2). Bateson extended this definition thus:

> We began by considering the relation between details of culture on the one hand and the needs and desires of the individual on the other. But we are now faced with the fact that we cannot guess at those needs and desires but must first deduce them from the emphases of the culture as a whole. Thus, if we isolate from pragmatic function the concept of *affective function* which we may define, rigidly, in terms of the relation between details of culture and the emotional needs of individuals, it follows that we must construct another category for the relationship between the emotional content of the particular detail of behaviour whose functions we are studying and the emotional emphases of the culture as a whole. This category of function I shall call *ethological;* and I shall use the word *ethos* to refer collectively to the emotional emphases of the culture. [1958:32]

Bateson argues that the ethos of a group, once established, becomes a very real factor in determining the conduct of the group's members and that an intimate relationship between ethos and cultural structure "is especially characteristic of small segregated groups where the ethos is uniform and the 'tradition' very much alive" (1958:121). Elsewhere ethos is referred to as the "specific tones of behaviour" which express "a standardised system of emotional attitudes" (1958:119).

Ethanol—the active ingredient in beverage alcohol—has become an integral part of the ethos of Greater Trukese Society, a group of communities where the ethos is uniform and the relevant tradition still very much alive. Ethanol has been woven so tightly into the very fabric of Trukese experience that it is difficult to imagine what Trukese culture would be like today had alcoholic beverages not been introduced. Through ingestion of ethanol young men carry out recurrent behaviors that express a standardized system of emotional attitudes about bravery, strength, aggression, and *machismo*. Ethanol may be viewed as the lubricant of contemporary Trukese ethos.

Thus the study of drunkenness in Truk is revealed to be something more: it is an investigation of what Bateson called an "ethological" category of function. Our study has allowed us to link the emotional needs of individuals (particularly young men) with the emotional emphases of

Trukese culture as a whole. By examining the relationship between ethos and ethanol we have gained insight into Trukese drunken comportment and, more importantly, into the prevalent emotional tone of Greater Trukese Society. Because the concept of *ethos* is closely linked with values and ideas about the nature of reality (see, e.g., Barnouw 1963), our focus on ethos and ethanol has given us a glimpse into the Trukese world view.

Postscript

Alcoholism in the sense of abnormal, addictive, pathologically compulsive intake of alcohol is not the same as drunkenness, which can be quite normal culturally.

> D. Mandelbaum, "Alcohol and culture"

If prevention is of equal importance with treatment, the social, cultural and psychological roles of alcohol must be understood.

> D. Horton, "The functions of alcohol in primitive societies: A cross-cultural study"

It has become fashionable to assert that alcoholism, or alcohol abuse, represents a major social problem in Micronesia today for which some solution must be found. For example, a U. S. government report on social services in the Trust Territory claims that programs in alcoholism and drug abuse are needed and that

> the alcoholism problem is particularly important. Training programs within the schools, community colleges, or adult education programs could have a salutory effect. Community-wide education programs, particularly in the district centers, along with funds for treatment and rehabilitation of individuals afflicted with alcoholism or alcohol abuse could be used immediately. [USDHEW 1973:27–28]

One of the first attempts toward accomplishing some of these goals in Truk during 1976 was a dismal failure. Films in English about American alcoholics were shown to groups of Trukese—most of whom could not understand English and many of whom were women—followed by a lengthy lecture during which the audience was discouraged from asking questions. Posters of the National Institute of Alcohol Abuse and Alcoholism decrying the misuse of alcohol appeared briefly in some of the downtown bars, but they, too, were in English and were ignored by most bar patrons. Despite Mahoney's (1974) perceptive statements that the heaviest drinking in Micronesia is indulged in by wage workers imbibing in the bars of the port towns, the general belief continues that Micronesia's major alcohol abusers are unemployed male high school dropouts in the district centers. This myth persists because the indicators taken to show the presence of severe, addictive alcoholism turn out to measure the style of drinking instead of the presence of addiction (cf. Levy and Kunitz 1974). This misapprehension is clearly the case for Truk.

In the Alcoholism Plan for the Trust Territory it is maintained that "problem drinking in Truk is primarily limited to males in the age group 16–25. Although drinking underage [sic] 21 itself constitutes a crime, other illegal and anti-social behavior associated with drinking is very much in evidence" (USTTPI 1975: Section on Truk; unnumbered pages). We are also told in this plan that these young male drinkers "possess an above-average education, but are generally on the fringes of the job market" and that "individuals in this same group whose only differing characteristic is that they hold fairly good jobs . . . are far less likely to get into trouble as a result of their drinking." Following these same lines, the 1976 update of the plan identifies two populations presumed to be at a high risk for developing alcohol-related problems: those persons between the ages of 15 and 26 who are neither in school nor employed, and those persons who reside away from home in order to attend school either in the district centers or outside Micronesia. Using data from my own field research in Greater Trukese Society I decided to examine each of these assumptions in more detail.

To begin with, I could discover no relationship between unemployment and drinking among young men in Peniyesene. Approximately one half of all village drinkers were unemployed at the time of my study, but they did not behave noticeably different when drunk from their more fortunate compatriots who had jobs. Employed or unemployed, Peniyesene young men drank with equal frequency, fought with equal fervor, and were equally likely to create drunken disturbances. Moreover, an examination of marital status, religious affiliation and educational history as potentially important variables also failed to reveal anything of interest. Only the variable "age of drinker" clearly demarcated those who participated in disruptive drinking in Peniyesene. When the ages of males actually involved in drunken fights during the period of my research were tallied, the following facts came to light: (1) less than one fifth of the 18- and 19-year-old drinkers engaged in brawling; (2) about two thirds of all drinkers between the ages of 20 and 29 participated in a physical altercation of some sort; and (3) less than one fifth of the 30- to 35-year-old drinkers took part in drunken fighting. It must be reemphasized that the employment status of these Peniyesene young men bore no relationship to their participation in "weekend warfare"; in fact, some of the "best and the bravest" of Peniyesene's warriors were employed in prestigious wage jobs.

Having thus exploded the myth that it is only the unemployed, poorly educated young man in Truk who drinks in a rowdy manner, I next turned to my Namoluk data to examine the suggestion that persons residing away from home in order to attend school in the district center are at a high risk of developing serious problems with alcohol. But once more nothing in my extensive data on Namoluk youth, who attend both Truk and Xavier High Schools in significant numbers, showed anything untoward about their encounter with alcoholic beverages. This finding was further supported by information I gathered on the drinking habits of other outer island youth attending school in the district center.

Thus the efforts of the Trust Territory's Alcoholism Plan to treat young male "juvenile delinquent" problem drinkers in Truk seem misdirected. This conclusion receives support from an unexpected quarter. Conducting a research project on the youth of Iras Village, Jack et al. first emphasized that village "trouble-makers" only made trouble when they were drunk and pointed out that "most drop-outs, *even unemployed dropouts*, do not have a reputation for being trouble-makers. *It would be a mistake to conclude that all or even most drop-outs become trouble-makers*" (1977:12; emphasis added). Unfortunately, it is just this mistaken conclusion that seems to guide the policies and alcohol treatment programs being planned for Truk and the other districts of the Trust Territory.

I believe that the reasons for this misdirection of official policy have their root in American values, especially in the Protestant work ethic that has figured so prominently in the history of the American people. The folk wisdom that derives from the Protestant ethic in the United States is that "hard work is its own reward." Americans continue to place great importance on diligent labor in the belief that those who work hard will be rewarded in this world, if not in the next. This emphasis on hard work, coupled with the belief that independence and responsibility should characterize all adults, clashes with the Trukese values on play, dependence, and irresponsibility for young men. Americans who come to Truk are greatly troubled at seeing able-bodied young men just sitting around. Many speak quite disparagingly of Trukese young men as a bunch of "lazy good-for-nothings who can't be trusted with any responsibility." They make much of the apparent fact that few young men contribute much time or labor to productive tasks benefiting their families, choosing instead to just idle about playing pool and getting horrendously drunk. These same Americans seem totally blind to the fact that they are judging these young men by an alien standard. Starting from a set of values grounded in the belief in the virtue of hard work, then, American commentators and policymakers have concluded that "the greatest problem in Micronesia today is the idleness of the young people" (USDHEW 1973:30) and that this leads inexorably to such delinquent behaviors as alcohol abuse.

By now the implications of my study for alcohol treatment programs in Truk should be obvious. Few if any young men in Greater Trukese Society drink in an addictive manner that could be labeled *alcoholism*. Although some adults in Truk are clearly addicted to ethanol, they do not come from the ranks of unemployed youth; rather they are to be found among the employed adult men. The ostentatious, obnoxious drunken comportment of Trukese young men is today inextricably interwoven with basic Trukese beliefs about strength, courage, and manhood. No amount of preaching about the evils of drink will be sufficient to wean young men from the gin bottle. We can state with total confidence that uninformed and misguided attempts to develop alcohol treatment programs for Trukese young men presumed to be suffering either from severe alcohol abuse or from addictive alcoholism will prove to be unmitigated failures. And the same can be said for the rest of Micronesia. More in-depth information on Micronesian drinking customs and values is needed before any meaningful and significant alcohol treatment programs can be established that will reach those few Micronesians who are truly in the thrall of demon rum.

136

Notes

CHAPTER 1

1. An atoll is an island type that occurs in tropical oceans. It consists of a string of low islets built up on a coral reef base surrounding an enclosed lagoon. Truk Atoll is unique in that numerous small, high volcanic islands are contained within its lagoon. This combination has given rise to its designation as a *complex atoll*.

2. Some foreigners who suffer from fungal conditions insist that Moen literally grows on you.

3. Trukese have borrowed *benjo* 'latrine' from the Japanese.

4. The boat pool is a parking lot for outboard motorboats from other islands in Truk Lagoon that voyage daily to Moen with a cargo of commuters and shoppers.

5. By comparison, Namoluk Atoll had twenty-two students enrolled in high school during 1975–1976 out of a total ethnic population of 458. In addition, while only three persons from Peniyesene were enrolled in college during 1975–1976, Namoluk boasted twenty-three, or 5 percent of its entire population.

6. The ownership of Mt. Winifëwürëër is contested, and this statement merely repeats the claims of Peniyesene persons.

7. These air raid shelters now serve as safe havens during the periodic typhoons that rake Truk.

8. The census I conducted in Peniyesene departs from a standard de facto census by counting anyone resident in the village for a week or more during the month of March 1976 as a member of the Peniyesene resident population. This departure from standard demographic practice was occasioned by my inability to get around to every household in the community on a single day and by the daily fluctuation in visitors who remained in the village for varying lengths of time.

9. The reader wishing a more comprehensive treatment of Trukese social organization is referred to Goodenough (1951) and Marshall (1972). Only those features of Trukese social organization directly pertinent to understanding drinking behavior in Peniyesene are introduced here.

10. I use the term *Greater Trukese Society* to refer to all the inhabited communities of Truk District, U. S. Trust Territory of the Pacific Islands. In this book, Truk is

often used as a synonym for Greater Trukese Society and I call all persons in this aggregation of communities "Trukese."

CHAPTER 2

1. Under German rule, only the chiefs were officially permitted to drink imported alcoholic beverages (U. S. Navy 1944:101). On many islands the German governor attempted, without notable success, to impose a ban on the manufacture of fermented coconut toddy (e.g., Born 1904:184).

2. I distinguish between *alcohol abuse* as socially disruptive behaviors associated with the consumption of beverage alcohol, and *alcoholism* as physiological or psychological dependency on ethanol which may or may not be accompanied by socially disruptive behaviors. According to this distinction, very few Trukese drinkers are alcoholics, although Truk has a great deal of alcohol abuse (see chapter 4 and Postscript).

3. Although the necessary historical research has yet to be undertaken, it seems likely that tobacco first reached Truk from the Spanish colony in the Marianas, carried by sailors from the Central Carolinian atolls who voyaged to both places.

4. See, for example, Wright and Fry (1936:309) who contend that the fulminations of the ABCFM missionaries in Hawaii in the 1830s "against pipe-smokers were almost as bitter as those against drunkards." Thorner finds emotional control to be of profound importance to all ascetic Protestants and claims that they experience misgivings over breaches in discipline in which submission to the "appetites" is interpreted as a sign of moral weakness. In Thorner's view, "tobacco and liquor are felt to be chinks in the armor of impulse control, faults that open the gate to delinquency and hinder social and moral improvement, impediments to the creation of the City of God on earth" (1953:169).

5. "Dread Hogoleu" is an old, alternative name for Truk Lagoon that reflects Truk's fearsome reputation among foreigners in the nineteenth century (see Preface).

6. Occasionally, persons in Greater Trukese Society were treated to alcoholic beverages early in the contact period, but these random events did not lead to subsequent traffic in spirits. See, for example, Nason's (1975:162) description of the Russian explorer Lütke treating the chief of Lukunor to madeira in 1828.

7. The Japanese made some effort to control drinking in Micronesia prior to 1921 with a set of Rules for the Control of Liquors in the South Sea Islands contained in Civil Administration Ordinance No. 2, issued in January 1916 (Japan 1931b:149). As far as I can tell, these rules were simply honored in the breach and were ineffective.

8. Sake is Japanese rice wine with a pure ethanol content of 14–16 percent. *Shochu* is a distilled liquor, often made from sweet potatoes, which ranges between 31 percent and 62 percent pure ethanol (Yamamuro 1958:487).

9. I have collapsed the two reported categories of "metals and metal goods" and "timber and wooden goods" into this single category for purposes of comparison with the 1969 material.

10. Such import figures for alcoholic beverages in the Pacific appear to be neither

new nor peculiar to the Trust Territory. Beverage alcohol represented 4.2 percent of all imports to the Kingdom of Tonga in 1887, at which time it ranked third in dollar value of all imports behind foodstuffs and building and construction materials (Government of Tonga 1888).

11. Yamamuro (1958:490) refers to persons from Okinawa and the other Ryūkyū Islands in much the same way: "The majority of them loved drinking and their morals were notoriously lax."

12. It is strange that palm wine is referred to here as "not very strong" in comparison with beer since we have already noted that it has an average pure ethanol content higher than many commercial beers. Also worthy of note is the reference to a style of drunken comportment that could as easily be Japanese as Trukese: "happy drunks who sing sentimental songs until they lapse into blissful slumber." This may reflect the influence of Japanese drinking models on Trukese drunken comportment.

13. While a majority of Trukese municipalities are dry, this should not be taken to mean that drinking does not occur in these communities (see Marshall 1975a; Nason 1975; Severance 1974).

14. In its first year the tax on beer alone accounted for one third of all district revenues. Joined with the income from taxes on cigarettes, beer and cigarette sales made up nearly one half (46 percent) of Truk District's total revenues in 1960 (Raken 1960:3).

15. This is a reference to a traditional weapon still sported by young Trukese males. It is made of a coil of wire to which shark's teeth are attached with heavy twine. The hand is then placed through the coil and made into a fist, whereupon the shark's teeth protrude menacingly from the user's knuckles.

16. The Japanese annual reports to the League of Nations maintain there were no bars, as such, in the territory and alcoholic beverages were sold either from retail outlets that carried a variety of other goods or at restaurants. At the end of 1931, fifteen persons were engaged in the sale of liquors in this manner in Truk; their number dropped to fourteen a year later and then rose to nineteen during 1933 and 1934 (Japan 1933:34, 1934:23, 1935:60, 1936:60).

17. Beginning on November 1, 1974, Truk District required all persons who wished to drink to possess an Alcoholic Beverage Consumption Identification Card. This card, issued by the Truk District Police Department, had a photograph of the bearer along with his name, height, and so forth, and was to be presented whenever package or over-the-counter alcoholic beverages were purchased. A drinking permit cost $6 for one year and could be obtained only by those age 21 or older. Originally, violators of this law could be fined up to $500 or imprisoned for up to six months or both; this fine was reduced to $100 by the District Legislature in 1975. The law is not well enforced and it is relatively easy to purchase liquor without a permit. As a revenue measure, however, this law has provided some new income for the district's coffers.

18. The Micronesian press recently reported that Congress of Micronesia Representative Lambert Aafin from Truk introduced a tongue-in-cheek resolution in the House of Representatives on January 23, 1978, urging that Truk be declared "a major disaster area" and asking that the U. S. Department of Agriculture act to

make surplus liquids available to Truk's people. The resolution went on to note that the "sudden drought" which struck Moen Island on January 15, 1978 "has parched the land and stricken the people with a great thirst for which there is no legal relief, spreading unhappiness and dismay even unto the outer islands" (*Marianas Variety News and Views* 1978).

CHAPTER 3

1. Many other Pacific Islanders employ variants of the native words for kava to describe alcoholic beverages (Lemert 1964:176). For example, Levy (1966:306) notes that Tahitians call alcoholic spirits *'ava no peritane* 'British kava'.

2. A variant of this home-brew that combines yeast with coconut juice has been described (Toomin and Toomin 1963:153, 172). This native brew sold on the black market in the mid-1950s for fifty cents a bottle.

3. When I conducted field work in Truk District during 1969–1971, Australian and French wines and a wide variety of beers and ales from New Zealand were on hand, the latter to slake the prodigious thirst of New Zealand construction workers then resident on Moen building the Continental Travelodge Hotel.

4. Elbert (1947) defines *wumwes* (*ümwes* in his orthography) as "crazy, troubled, puzzled, hoaxed, foolish, silly." My informants used only the first two meanings when describing drunks.

5. Writing about the Molima and Dobuans of the D'Entrecasteaux Islands off the east tip of New Guinea, Chowning (1961) and Fortune (1963) describe a closely related condition which they call "amok." In Molima, amok is viewed as a special type of insanity in which, among other things, the victim "cannot hear or understand what is said to him" (Chowning 1961:79). In both Dobu and Molima, "running amok is the one way to offer violence to neighbors without penalty," and in Molima, "running amok permits a person to exhibit the behavior of a warrior toward everyone . . . without responsibility for his actions. Not only is the sufferer not blamed, but his behavior is not condemned in any way" (Chowning 1961:80–81). Finally, from Fortune's description of his personal encounter with a "man amuck," it is clear that the violence associated with this condition is selective and not utterly unrestrained (Fortune 1963:54–55).

6. Newman (1964: 6–7) states that among the Gururumba, "wild-man behavior is limited exclusively to males between approximately 25 and 35 years of age." Clarke's (1973) review of the wild-man literature shows this generally to be the case elsewhere in New Guinea. The most striking exception to the young male wild-man syndrome is in Frankel's (1976) account of an outbreak among the Telefomin in which all but a single case of those affected were young women with a mean age of 18 years.

7. The most detailed probe into the Trukese system of values has been provided by Caughey (1970). I rely heavily on his research in this section. Caughey points out that significant differences appear to exist in the values of Wuumaan (the island he studied) and those of Romónum (where most other researchers have worked in Truk Lagoon). These differences cannot be adequately explained as attributes of

the cultural division between Nomwoneyas and Faaychuk (roughly the eastern and western halves of Truk Lagoon) since Toon, which is in Faaychuk along with Romónum, is described by Caughey as sharing the same values as Wuumaan, which is located in Nomwoneyas. My own field research on Namoluk Atoll in the Mortlocks and on Moen in Nomwoneyas indicates that the system of values described by Caughey is operative in these communities. This observation receives additional support from Nason (1975) and Severance (1975, 1976), both of whom conducted research elsewhere in the Mortlocks. While some local variation in emphasis probably exists in the ways these particular values apply in the different communities of Greater Trukese Society, I conclude that available evidence shows them to represent a general, widely shared paradigm that holds throughout the area.

8. Trukese base a great many things on performance. Elsewhere (Marshall 1977) I have shown that Trukese notions of kinship are founded first and foremost on the performance of nurturant acts.

9. It is not at all far-fetched to suggest that Logan's peculiar effectiveness with Trukese resulted from his embodying the ideal character traits of bravery and respectfulness. Logan had fought and been wounded in the American Civil War, and he showed no fear of striding into the midst of Trukese battles in an effort to break them up. This boldness resided in a man described as "unprejudiced," and "scrupulously fair, and often forgiving, in his treatment of natives" (Aberley 1975:28).

10. Although Trukese may have quickly taken to baseball as a surrogate for their own warlike propensities, it is significant that they were introduced to this game by the Japanese. Writing recently about baseball in Japan, Whiting (1977) argues that the game is played there in accordance with the ancient Samurai code of *Bushido* and that managers demand that players act like warriors both on and off the field. The Japanese home-run king, Sadaharu Oh, is even reported to practice his swing using a *katana*, or traditional long sword.

11. In addition to warfare and baseball, interlineage rivalry was expressed in competitive feasts of the sort described by Bollig (1927). Such rivalry also was exhibited during *töchap*, special "daring contributions" introduced in connection with a new savings system (Mahony 1960).

12. Open ocean voyages in sailing canoes are still regularly made in the western and Namonuito portions of Truk District (see map 5 and Gladwin 1970). Some islanders apparently increase the riskiness of these trips by adding alcohol to the equation, although it appears that these "drunken sailors" are probably not as drunk as they let on: "Parties frequently set sail from Puluwat to Pikelot [a distance of over 100 miles] on the spur of the moment, while drunk on palm toddy. They always arrive" (Lewis 1974:775–776).

13. Peniyesene young men materially heightened this risk during mid-May 1976 by racing around outside while drinking yeast in the midst of Typhoon Pamela. This was done in open defiance of the district administrator's orders to remain inside and to refrain from drinking alcoholic beverages, and at considerable risk to life and limb.

14. This cry translates literally as "Canoe-ho!" or "Sail-ho!" but it is used commonly throughout the area to gain public attention when one is angry or when a

fight is about to begin. On outer islands, such as Namoluk, this cry is uttered whenever a canoe, motorboat, ship, or aircraft is sighted.

15. This masculine exclusivity in regard to alcohol is widespread in Oceania (see, e.g., Hocking 1970; Lemert 1964, 1976; Marshall and Marshall 1975; Ogan 1966; Schmidt 1970; Schwartz and Romanucci-Ross 1974).

16. The youngest known drinker during my field work in Peniyesene was 18 years old, but many young men are known to take their first drink between 14 and 18 years of age. Very few young men become regular drinkers until at least age 18.

17. The association of tobacco with alcohol as strong substances is culturally significant. Men without cigarettes are referred to as *apwangapwang* 'weak', 'lacking strength'. Conversely, those who use cigarettes are believed to possess the opposite and valued trait of strength, which Trukese believe to be enhanced by tobacco.

18. Compare Simmons (1960:1024), who maintains that in Lunahuaná "to drink is to conform to a normal pattern of the group's culture." The same is true for drinking by young men in Truk.

19. This is much like the behavior reported for the Navajo by Levy and Kunitz (1974:185): "Navajo males tend to drink heavily in their younger years and to either stop completely or to decrease their intake considerably after middle age."

CHAPTER 4

1. Given the public and social character of Trukese drinking, I am confident that these figures accurately reflect the number of drinkers in Peniyesene during the research period. These figures emphatically are not an enumeration of problem drinkers or alcoholics.

2. Nevertheless, his older unemployed brother was a regular drinker.

3. The *mwichen asor* 'meeting with the supernatural' (in this case the Christian God) is a regular service program run by the Catholic mission throughout much of Truk Lagoon. It is closely patterned after similar programs sponsored by various Protestant groups elsewhere in the Pacific, for example, the Blue Cross in French Polynesia (see Kay 1963: 350–351; cf. also Schwartz and Romanucci-Ross 1974:218). The aim of these programs is to get persons to forswear alcoholic beverages and/or tobacco for a specified length of time. In Truk, *mwichen asor* rotate monthly from community to community throughout the year. I attended one such meeting hosted by Peniyesene on Sunday, March 7, 1976. Following a small feast, a series of hortatory speeches was given by native church leaders (nearly all of whom were adult men) who stressed the evils of drink and urged those present to pledge themselves before God to abstain for several months at minimum. Interspersed among these speeches were songs sung by groups of young people from different villages, all of which dwelt on the theme that alcohol causes nothing but trouble. After about two hours of speeches and music, the Catholic priest asked those who would offer a pledge of abstention to God to step forward, had them repeat the pledge after him, blessed the gathering, and the meeting adjourned. While the *mwichen asor* seems to help a few Trukese stay away from liquor, it does not appear to be overly successful in reaching a majority of those who drink, namely, the young men. Sig-

nificantly, of the thirty or so men who took the pledge at the meeting I attended in Peniyesene, none was from the host village.

4. Jellinek sorts alcoholism into several species, of which gamma alcoholism is considered the most serious. Gamma alcoholism involves acquired tissue tolerance to alcohol; adaptive cell metabolism; withdrawal symptoms; and craving, that is, physical dependence on ethanol and loss of control over drinking. Jellinek observes that "the damage to health in general and to financial and social standing are [*sic*] also more prominent than in other species of alcoholism" (1960:37).

5. Truk High School has a rule that the first time a student is caught drinking or drunk he is campused and put on probation; the second time, he is kicked out of school. The junior high schools in Truk District and Xavier High School have similar rules governing the use of alcohol by their students.

6. This was the only time I saw a Peniyesene female drink. Significantly, old men and women become sociologically neuter for some purposes. In addition, this particular woman was viewed as an eccentric by many in the village. The only other Peniyesene female reported to have consumed alcohol (who was not in Truk during my stay) had been away to school in the United States for several years and supposedly acquired her drinking habit there. See chapter 5 for a more detailed discussion of Trukese attitudes toward women and alcohol.

7. Many well-meaning but misguided and ethnocentric foreigners assume that young men in Truk drink more these days than formerly because today no one punishes them for their drunken misbehavior. "All they need is some good firm discipline," runs this argument. This lamentable leniency is then put up to acculturation pressures which, we are told, somehow have led to the breakdown of family and community controls over young people. I argue in chapters 7 and 8 that this view is untenable.

8. That the game of death goes on is revealed by a letter I received from Father Francis Hezel in March 1977, from which the following extract is taken:

> Last Sunday there was a Penia boy killed in a knife fight with another boy from the same village. I just missed seeing the killing myself. I was running with two Xavier boys past Peniasene when a car with the victim and several others on it sped past on the way to the hospital. Apparently the stabbing happened just after we crossed the Penia bridge near the *uut* in Penia. The victim died that evening and the boy who killed him reportedly turned himself in to the police. Both were related to one of our seniors here. Incidentally, this is the first homicide in several months of which I am aware, although there have been three more suicides since my article on the subject was published—a Sapuk youth a month and a half ago, an Iras boy in early February, and a Truk High senior from Tol just two weeks ago. . . . All these follow the typical pattern that I described in my article.
>
> XYZ is the name of the boy killed. Word has it that he had insulted and even physically assaulted the father of ABC before Christmas. In retribution, various members of the insulted party's family had beaten XYZ since then—to the point where it had gotten to be the expected thing in the village. Last Sunday ABC was doing just that (under the influence of alcohol, of course) when XYZ took off his belt and gave ABC a few good lashes with it. ABC seemingly lost his head and stabbed XYZ in the arm

143

cutting an artery. When XYZ went to the ground, ABC began to systematically stab him from the legs up to the throat area. ABC's brother, MNO, was also involved in the incident and stoned XYZ after he had been stabbed, not aware of the extent of the injuries that he had already suffered. When MNO came closer and saw that XYZ was in bad shape, he dragged his older brother away. Meanwhile, the by-standers took XYZ to the hospital where he died sometime that same day.

During the funeral, ABC and his brother were locked in their house for their own protection. Shortly afterwards they both turned themselves in to the police and are now awaiting trial in the local jail.

9. Newman (1964:6) mentions a New Guinea wild man he observed who spoke exclusively in Neo-Melanesian (a language not normally spoken among the Gururumba) while possessed.

CHAPTER 5

1. Significantly, masculinity is associated with the right-hand side in Truk, the side of strength, *peni emwään;* femininity is linked with the left-hand, soft, or weak side, *peni emmöng.* The word *mwään* itself may be used to refer to the right-hand side, and the word *feefin* may be used for the left (see, e.g., Elbert 1947).

2. There are internal differences within Greater Trukese Society regarding certain aspects of food preparation. For example, all over Truk Lagoon it is considered men's work to beat taro or breadfruit into a pastelike consistency (called *kon*) with a stone pounder. In the Mortlocks this task is assigned only to women.

3. The greater presence of women in church seems to be a pattern of long standing in Greater Trukese Society. The Reverend Robert Logan, describing a trip to the Mortlocks in 1887, commented that "at many of the islands the [church] schools are composed very largely of girls and young women," and the church school on Losap was described as having "but few boys or young men in it" (ABCFM 1888:12, 15).

4. It is notable that women all over the Pacific have been at the forefront of opposition to the sale of intoxicating liquors. Richard (1957*b*:488–489) reports that in the spring of 1950 "a group of Palauan women presented a lucid petition entitled 'The Evil of Drink' " to a United Nations Visiting Mission calling at Koror. When the proposal was first made to legalize drinking in Papua New Guinea in the 1950s, "witnesses against the proposal included a delegation of native women who said that such a measure would result in poverty and degradation of the Native people, and asked that prohibition be continued" (Anonymous 1956:209). More recently, Ponapean women marched in the streets of Kolonia in an effort to keep the bars closed after they were temporarily shut down by the district administrator in July 1971 following a drunken homicide (*Micronitor* 1971). Although no formal public demonstration by women against alcohol has occurred in Truk, women were quite vociferous in telling me of their opposition to liquor, in keeping with their public image as "saintly" persons. More significantly, though, it was reportedly the church women's groups in Truk who were mainly behind two bills drafted but never formally introduced to the Truk District Legislature during 1976. The first of these bills would have reinstituted total prohibition. The second sought to prohibit all imports of alcoholic beverages while still permitting local manufacture. Women reportedly voted heavily in favor of Moen's recently instituted prohibition law (see chapter 2).

5. This clear distinction between the sexes is widespread in Micronesia (see, e.g., Alkire 1968).

6. A young Namoluk man of my acquaintance was angry with his older sister who had recently returned to Truk from two years of college in the United States because of the "wrong" and "bad" ideas she had acquired in America concerning women's roles. He was especially incensed over her stated intent to go play pool in the poolhalls.

7. The very few Trukese women who drink either do so surreptitiously and in private so as not to sully their public reputations for respectability or they are bar girls. Bar girls serve as waitresses and dance partners in the downtown drinking establishments, and many of them consume alcoholic beverages. In the public expectation *all* bar girls drink and are loose women, and any woman who takes such a job risks being viewed as fair game by male bar patrons. No Peniyesene women worked as bar girls at the time of my research.

8. Young women are not explicitly given the reasons I have just outlined for why they should not drink. Instead they are indoctrinated with the notion that drinking by women is *meyi ngau* 'bad' or 'wrong'; *aseu* 'shameful', 'humiliating', 'embarrassing'; and that it *atana euranian Chuuk seni nom* 'violates traditional Trukese custom'. Informants agree that drinking by women would be scandalous because when drunk women might, for example, use forbidden language within earshot of male kin or expose their private parts to public view by ripping off their clothes. The general picture that emerges is that females should not imbibe alcohol because this would precipitate immodest and immoral behavior on their part.

9. One wonders how much influence the Japanese concept of *face* had on the comparable Trukese notion. My own belief is that it simply served to reinforce this preexisting element in Trukese culture.

10. One informant stressed to me that he would be ashamed to have his wife employed for wages if he too were not so employed since she would then have shown herself stronger than he.

11. This is an interesting inversion of the American notion that whoever reaches orgasm first wins in the sense of achieving greater satisfaction.

12. Before the inroads of Christianity put an end to the performance of most traditional dances in Greater Trukese Society, dancing offered a major alternative public setting for a young man to display his charms to women: "Various groups of young men vied with each other in undertaking ever more complex combination of motions and shifts in position of partners, along with increasing speed, as they were inspired by the admiration of the audience" (Gladwin and Sarason 1953:105).

CHAPTER 6

1. Out of the 125 societies that Horton originally surveyed for his sample, 26 were drawn from the "Oceania" category as it appears in the Yale Cross-Cultural Survey and its descendant, the Human Relations Area Files. Horton recognized that information on alcohol use in this region of the world was scarce (1943:237). Of these 26 societies, only 2 (Maori and Murngin) yielded adequate data to be included for Horton's purposes (see also Marshall 1976a).

2. This assumption has since proved false. Gathering and hunting societies now are recognized by anthropologists to provide a secure food base for their members. At least one such group has even been labeled "the original affluent society" (*Time Magazine* 1969; see also Lee 1968).

3. The Mortlock Islands, for example, suffered extensive devastation and loss of local food resources in major typhoons that struck in 1907 and again in May 1976 (see Marshall 1976c regarding the 1976 storm).

4. Mahoney apparently failed to consider that the Marianas District is demographically heterogeneous on account of the present location of the capital of the Trust Territory on Saipan. Substantial numbers of persons from every district in Micronesia may be found on Saipan, along with expatriates from the United States and the Philippines. The presence of all these non-Chamorros no doubt has had some effect on the violent crime ratio.

5. The first Protestant missionaries went to the Marshalls in 1857, and traders did not move into these islands until the 1860s and 1870s. In Yap and Palau, traders became active at approximately the same time although permanent missionization, in this case by Catholics, did not take place until 1886 in Yap and 1891 in Palau (Hezel 1970).

6. *Pacific Islands* is here limited to Polynesia, Melanesia, Micronesia, and New Guinea and does not correspond to the "Oceania" category in the Human Relations Area Files which includes aboriginal Australia and much of Island Southeast Asia.

7. I base this assertion on the following facts: in three cases (Arapesh; Ontong Java; Wogeo), BBC are unable to say anything about alcohol, even including whether it was present or absent; in another eight cases (Lau, Fiji; Buka; Kwoma; Malaita; Vanua Levu; Tikopia; Trobriands; Marquesas), all BBC can determine is whether or not beverage alcohol was used aboriginally or postcontact. In yet another eight cases (Carolinians; Chamorro; Lesu; Manus; Nauruans; Pukapuka; Samoans; Trukese), BBC are able to code only ten or less of the possible ninety-seven items in their tables (Bacon, Barry, Child, and Snyder 1965).

8. *Carolinians* here refers to the descendants of voyagers from the central Carolinian atolls who settled on Saipan in the Marianas Islands during the eighteenth century.

9. If one chooses to emphasize peculiarities rather than similarities it might be possible to argue that most, if not all, island communities in Greater Trukese Society represent different cultures. I have chosen to treat all these communities as one for analytic purposes, not because I am blind to the very real internal variation that occurs in Greater Trukese Society, but rather because I believe more progress can be made in understanding Trukese culture in this way. While Namoluk Atoll is comparable to, say, Ifaluk in scale and degree of differentiation from surrounding societies, I would deem it most inappropriate to have separate Human Relations Area Files on Namoluk and Truk, as if these were mutually exclusive cultural entities.

10. It may be significant that a drunk *can* predict the responses of others to his acts and furthermore that he knows he will not normally be punished for what he does while intoxicated.

11. Compare Hamer's (1969) material on the Potawatomi where child training and weaning are nearly identical to Truk but where, in line with BBC's theory, both men and women drink heavily.

CHAPTER 7

1. Compare Edgerton's account of a similar experience while doing field work with the Kamba in Kenya: Confronted by a drunken berserker who was attacking all whom he met, "much to my surprise, the man calmed down, and as he walked slowly past me, he greeted me in polite, even deferential terms, before he turned and dashed away" (MacAndrew and Edgerton 1969:64). Reo Fortune's record of an encounter with a "man amuck" on Dobu armed with a spear echoes Edgerton's experience:

> In this case the village did not consider me in their mad scurry. But after all there was no reason why they should. I was a stranger amongst them. And as it turned out I emerged unscathed. The man amuck was my own interpreter and he did not strike, though he stuffed earth into his mouth in horrid pantomime of eating me, still foaming, writhing, and threatening me as I trussed him up with rope after he was disarmed. [1963:55]

2. One day as I stood with a man in his late forties watching the latest scene in the ongoing drama of drunkenness in Peniyesene, he volunteered to me that many young men begin to behave in a bizarre manner after only one or two swigs of liquor before they are really drunk. He found this subterfuge humorous.

3. In keeping with this interpretation, Chowning (1961:81) insists that "any full explanation of amok must take into account the psychological strains engendered by each culture."

4. Mohatt (1972:273) explicitly acknowledges the same process to be at work among the Teton Sioux: "Like many Indian boys, John remembered taking his first drink at around 14 years of age. The way he acted after this first drink shows the influence on him of those he had seen drink. . . . The only way he knew how to act was the way he had seen others act."

5. This does not mean that all drinking by young Trukese men outside Truk is peaceful and unlike their drunken comportment at home. On the contrary, a substantial number of young men who have gone away to further their educations have gotten into serious trouble when drinking and fighting. Many have been expelled from school and sent home.

6. Other Carolinian societies appear to follow a similar pattern. For example, Burrows writes of Ifaluk Atoll that "on rare occasions, under extreme stress, a man may find relief in violence. (I say a man, because no instance was found of a woman doing it. Children, yes; but before they are enculturated.) Even then the rule of non-aggression has sway; for the violence is directed not against people, but against houses" (1952:24).

7. As we have seen (chapter 4, case 10) drunken young men may aggress against their parents on occasion by killing themselves in retaliation for real or imagined grievances.

CHAPTER 8

1. One of the four societies in the sample of Child, Barry, and Bacon that was an exception to the general trend allowing both sexes to drink alcoholic beverages was Ifaluk Atoll. Ifaluk is culturally and linguistically quite closely related to the islands of Greater Trukese Society and has had a very similar contact history with the outside world.

2. Carrying their speculation further, Gladwin and Sarason suggest that "penis envy does not exist among the Trukese, and might even have its analogue in this society in what might be called 'vagina envy' " (1953:255).

Glossary of Trukese Words

achi   Fermented coconut toddy; sour toddy; palm wine.

akapas   [Mortlockese dialect of Trukese] "war cry"; a cry used to gain public attention.

akurang   War cry (same as *akapas*).

angangan anuön   Young men's work; used in reference to drinking and crazy drunken comportment.

anuön   Young men roughly between the ages of 15 and 35 years.

apwangapwang   Weak; lacking strength.

aseu   Shameful; humiliating; embarrassing.

ät   Boys roughly between the ages of 3 and 14 years.

atana euranian Chuuk seni nom   Violates traditional Trukese custom.

chienap   Old person; elderly.

chon Peniyesene   The people, or citizens, of Peniyesene Village.

chon sakau   Drunks; inebriated persons.

ekiyek pwëcëkkün   Strong thought (see *ekiyekin mwään*).

ekiyek pwoteete   Weak thought (see *ekiyekin feefin*).

ekiyekin feefin   Womanly thought.

ekiyekin mwään   Manly thought.

epino   Hand net for fishing used by women.

fääl   Mortlockese dialect of Trukese; men's house; canoe house (see *uut*).

faapwin   Young woman.

feefin   Adult woman; mature woman.

itang   Religious-magical-military experts in traditional Trukese culture.

itenipwin   Love songs.

kek A practice between sweethearts in which the glowing end of a cigarette is used to burn the partner on the arms or chest as a sign of devotion and affection.

kon Pounded breadfruit or taro.

meyi ngau Bad; wrong; undesirable.

meyi pwich Hot; burning. Used in reference to distilled alcoholic beverages.

meyi wumwes Crazy; troubled; insane.

meyi wussun chëk maan Just like an animal.

monukön Infant of either sex.

mosonoson Respectfulness; kindness. Also used to describe a happy, quiet drunk.

mwään Adult man; mature man roughly between the ages of 35 and 60 years.

mwääneson A person who combines bravery with arrogance; a haughtily aggressive man.

mwichen asor A regular temperance meeting sponsored by the Catholic mission in Truk in which men take pledges before God to abstain from alcohol, tobacco, or both for specified lengths of time.

namanam tekia Arrogance; haughtiness; acting better than others.

nanchaku A two-sectional staff joined with a length of chain used as a weapon in Truk by weekend warriors.

nekenek A practice between sweethearts in which one or more cuts are made on the arm or chest with a knife or sharp piece of shell as a sign of devotion and affection.

nenien mwään Men's place; male turf. Used in reference to modern poolhalls and bars.

niköpwöt A practice between sweethearts in which the glowing end of a coconut leaflet midrib was used to burn the partner on the arms or chest as a sign of devotion and affection. Cigarette butts have now almost entirely replaced coconut leaflet midribs in this practice.

nissimwa Cowardice; weakness.

nömuti A practice between sweethearts during coital foreplay in which either partner may scratch the other on the side of the neck or on the buttocks with the fingernails.

peni emmöng Left-hand side; weak side.

peni emwään Right-hand side; strong side.

pio From the English word *beer*.

pwääng A traditional system of judo and jujitsu-like throws and holds used in warfare and self-defense.

pwara   Bravery; power; general competence.

pwiipwi   A general term for siblings; specifically, a created sibling.

pwiipwi winisam   Persons who are siblings by virtue of being descended from males of the same lineage, subclan, or clan.

ranin fäl   Sunday.

ranin fiyu   Day of fighting.

rese tongeni rongorong   They cannot hear or understand [what is said to them].

rong   Esoteric lore; knowledge.

sakau   Alcoholic beverages; the state of drunkenness. From the Ponapean word for *kava*.

säwa   A fishing basket used by women to store their catch.

soulang   A Christian or saintly person.

tamatsuki   Pocket billiards; pool. Loanword from Japanese.

tempura   Large, deep-fried doughnuts. Loanword from Japanese.

tiperoch   Unschooled; ignorant; stupid.

tipetchem   Educated; intelligent; smart.

töchap   Special competitive contributions made at public meetings.

uain   Wine. From the English word *wine*.

uut   Men's house; canoe house (see *fääl*).

wech/wechewech   Hit; strike; strike repeatedly.

wechewechen Chuuk   Trukese striking; a method of sexual intercourse in which the man endeavors to bring a woman to orgasm by repeatedly prodding her clitoris with his erect penis.

wesewesen pwara   True bravery; the combination of *pwara* and *mosonoson;* the ideal character type in Trukese culture.

wisiki   Distilled spirits. From the English word *whiskey*.

wussun monukön   Just like a baby or infant.

yiis   Home-brew. From the English word *yeast*.

Appendix

ARTICLE 1.

The term "liquors," as used in these Regulations, mean spirits and alcoholic beverages containing 3 per cent. or over of alcohol.

ARTICLE 2.

Liquors shall not be sold, nor bartered, nor given to the natives, nor shall the natives drink liquors, provided that this does not apply to persons who have the permit provided for in Article 7.

ARTICLE 3.

Natives shall not manufacture, nor buy and sell, nor give or take over, nor possess liquors.

ARTICLE 4.

When persons other than the natives desire to engage in the manufacture of liquors, such persons shall apply for permission to the Director of the Civil Administration Department; and when persons other than the natives desire to engage in the sale of liquors, the application for permission shall be made to the Chief of the Civil Administration Station.

153

ARTICLE 5.

Natives shall not drink liquors.

ARTICLE 6.

The Chief of the Civil Administration Station may permit the drinking of liquors by the natives in the following cases:

1. When liquors are needed for medical purposes, this being certified by the physician.
2. When liquors are needed for religious and other ceremonies and functions.

ARTICLE 7.

When the Chief of the Civil Administration Station has permitted a native to drink liquors, he will grant a permit for the drinking of liquors.

ARTICLE 8.

The permit provided for in the preceding Article shall not be used by persons other than the person for whom it has been granted.

ARTICLE 9.

Persons who have violated the provisions of Articles 2 to 5 and Article 8 shall be fined a sum not exceeding ¥150, and in the case of Article 3 the liquors concerned shall be confiscated.

Source: Japan 1924:26–27.

Bibliography

Aberley, J. 1975. "Robert W. Logan, the 'soldier-saint' of Micronesia." B.A. honors thesis, Australian National University, Canberra.

Akapito, C.; Anselmo, D.; Kuban, J. K.; Lirow, P.; and Tauwl, L. 1975. "Recreational business on Moen." Senior town project, Xavier High School, Moen, Truk. Copy on file in Micronesian Seminar Library, Moen, Truk, Eastern Caroline Islands.

Alkire, W. H. 1968. "Porpoises and taro." *Ethnology* 7(3): 280–89.

American Board of Commissioners for Foreign Missions (ABCFM). 1888. *Last Words and Work of Rev. Robt. W. Logan, a Missionary of the A.B.C.F.M. at Ruk, Micronesia. Together with Memorial Papers.* Oakland, California: Pacific Press Publishing Co. (Copy on file in B. P. Bishop Museum Library, Honolulu, Hawaii, DU Pac. Pam. 1042).

Anonymous. 1956. "Supply of liquor to New Guinea natives." *South Pacific* (Australian School of Pacific Administration) 8(10): 209–11.

Bacon, M. K., Barry, H. III; and Child, I. L. 1965. "A cross-cultural study of drinking: II. Relations to other features of culture." *Quarterly Journal of Studies on Alcohol*, Supplement No. 3. pp. 29–48.

Bacon, M. K.; Barry, H. III; Child, I. L.; and Snyder, C. R. 1965. "A cross-cultural study of drinking: V. Detailed definitions and data." *Quarterly Journal of Studies on Alcohol.* Supplement No. 3. pp. 78–111.

Barnouw, V. 1963. *Culture and Personality.* Homewood, Illinois: The Dorsey Press.

Bates, M., and Abbott, D. P. 1958. *Coral Island: Portrait of an Atoll.* New York: Charles Scribner's Sons.

Bateson, G. 1958. *Naven.* 2nd ed. Stanford, California: Stanford University Press.

Benedict, R. 1967. *The Chrysanthemum and the Sword. Patterns of Japanese Culture.* Cleveland and New York: World Publishing Co.

Berreman, G. 1956. "Drinking patterns of the Aleuts." *Quarterly Journal of Studies on Alcohol* 17: 503–14.

Bishop, Rev. S. E. 1888. "Missionary life of Mr. Logan." In *Last Words and Work of Rev. Robt. W. Logan, a Missionary of the A.B.C.F.M. at Ruk, Micronesia. Together with Memorial Papers.* Oakland, California: Pacific Press Publishing Co.

155

Bollig, P. 1927 *Die Bewohner der Truk-Inseln: Religion, Leben und Kurze Grammatik eines Mikronesiervolkes. Anthropos* 3(1). Internationale Sammlung Ethnologischer Monographien. Münster: Aschendorffsche Verlagsbuchhandlung.

Born, L. 1904. "Einige Beobachtungen ethnographischer Natur über die Oleai-Inseln." *Mitteilungen aus den Deutschen Schutzgebeiten* 17: 175–91. (English translation No. 1185 on file in Pacific Collection, Gregg Sinclair Library, University of Hawaii.)

Brown, R. G. 1976. "The German acquisition of the Caroline Islands: 1898–99." In *Germany in the Pacific and Far East: 1870–1914*, edited by J. A. Moses and P. M. Kennedy, pp. 137–55. St. Lucia: University of Queensland Press.

Burrows, E. G. 1952. "From value to ethos on Ifaluk Atoll." *Southwestern Journal of Anthropology* 8(1): 13–35.

Burrows, E. G. and Spiro, M. E. 1957. *An Atoll Culture. Ethnography of Ifaluk in the Central Carolines*. New Haven: Human Relations Area Files.

Caughey, F. B. 1971. "The social context of pregnancy and childbirth on Uman, Truk." Master's thesis, University of Pennsylvania.

Caughey, J. L. III. 1970. "Cultural values in a Micronesian society." Ph.D. dissertation, University of Pennsylvania.

Cheyne, A. 1852. *A Description of Islands in the Western Pacific Ocean North and South of the Equator: With Sailing Directions, Together with Their Productions; Manners and Customs of the Natives and Vocabularies of Their Various Languages*. London: J. D. Potter.

Child, I. L.; Barry, H. III; and Bacon, M. K. 1965. "A cross-cultural study of drinking: III. Sex differences." *Quarterly Journal of Studies on Alcohol*, Supplement No. 3. pp. 49–61.

Chowning, A. 1961. "Amok and aggression in the D'Entrecasteaux." In *Proceedings of the 1961 Annual Spring Meeting of the American Ethnological Society, Symposium: Patterns of Land Utilization and Other Papers*, edited by V. E. Garfield, pp. 78–83. Seattle: University of Washington Press.

Clarke, W. C. 1973. "Temporary madness as theatre: Wild-man behaviour in New Guinea." *Oceania* 43(3): 198–214.

Clifton, J. A. 1964. "The acceptance of external political controls on Truk and Ponape." *International Journal of Comparative Sociology* (Leiden) 5(1): 91–103.

Curley, R. T. 1967. "Drinking patterns of the Mescalero Apache." *Quarterly Journal of Studies on Alcohol* 28: 116–31.

Dailey, R. C. 1968. "The role of alcohol among North American Indian tribes as reported in the Jesuit Relations." *Anthropologica*, n.s., 10(1): 45–57.

Dennis, P. A. 1975. "The role of the drunk in a Oaxacan village." *American Anthropologist* 77(4): 856–63.

Des Moines Register. 1977. Editorial entitled "We're No. 1!" April 17, 1977.

Doane, Rev. E. T. 1881. "The Lagoon of Ruk." *Missionary Herald* 77: 208–210.

Dore, R. P. 1967. *City Life in Japan. A Study of a Tokyo Ward*. Berkeley and Los Angeles: University of California Press.

Elbert, S. H. 1947. *Trukese-English and English-Trukese Dictionary, with Notes on*

156

Pronunciation, Grammar, Vocabularies, Phrases. Pearl Harbor: U.S. Naval Military Government.

Everett, M. W. n.d. "Drinking" and "trouble": the Apachean experience. Unpublished manuscript.

Field, P. B. 1962. "A new cross-cultural study of drunkenness." In *Society, Culture, and Drinking Patterns*, edited by D. J. Pittman and C. R. Snyder, pp. 48–74. New York: John Wiley & Sons.

Firth, S. 1973. "German firms in the Western Pacific Islands: 1857–1914." *Journal of Pacific History* 8: 10–28.

Fischer, A. 1950. *The Role of the Trukese Mother and its Effect on Child Training.* SIM Report No. 8. Washington, D.C.: Pacific Science Board, National Research Council.

Fischer, J. L., and Swartz, M. J. 1960. "Socio-psychological aspects of some Trukese and Ponapean love songs." *Journal of American Folklore* 73: 218–224.

Fortune, R. F. 1963. *Sorcerers of Dobu.* New York: E. P. Dutton & Co.

Frankel, S. 1976. "Mass hysteria in the New Guinea Highlands. A Telefomin outbreak and its relationship to other New Guinea hysterical reactions." *Oceania* 47(2): 106–33.

Geertz, C. 1973. "Thick description: Toward an interpretive theory of culture." In Geertz, C. *The Interpretation of Cultures: Selected Essays*, pp. 3–30. New York: Basic Books.

Girschner, M. 1912. "Die Karoleninsul Namoluk und ihre Bewohner." *Baessler-Archiv* 2: 123–215.

Gladwin, T. 1953. "The role of man and woman on Truk: a problem in personality and culture." *Transactions of the New York Academy of Sciences*, series 2, 15: 305–309.

———. 1958. "Canoe travel in the Truk area: Technology and its psychological correlates." *American Anthropologist* 60(5): 893–99.

———. 1970. *East is a Big Bird. Navigation and Logic on Puluwat Atoll.* Cambridge: Harvard University Press.

Gladwin, T., and Sarason, S. B. 1953. *Truk: Man in Paradise.* Viking Fund Publications in Anthropology, No. 20. New York: Wenner-Gren Foundation for Anthropological Research, Inc.

Glaessner, V. 1974. *Kung Fu. Cinema of Vengeance.* New York: Bounty Books.

Gluckman, L. K. 1974. "Alcohol and the Maori in historical perspective." *The New Zealand Medical Journal* 79(506): 553–55.

Goodenough, W. H. 1949. "Premarital freedom on Truk: theory and practice." *American Anthropologist* 51(4): 615–20.

———. 1951. *Property, Kin, and Community on Truk.* Yale University Publications in Anthropology, No. 46. New Haven: Yale University Press.

———. 1965. "Rethinking 'status' and 'role': Toward a general model of the cultural organization of social relationships." In *The Relevance of Models for Social Anthropology*, edited by M. Banton, pp. 1–24. ASA Monograph No. 1. London: Tavistock Publications.

————. 1966. "Human purpose in life." *Zygon, Journal of Religion and Science* 1(3): 217–29.

Gorad, S. L.; McCourt, W. F.; and Cobb, J. C. 1971. "A communications approach to alcoholism." *Quarterly Journal of Studies on Alcohol* 32: 651–68.

Hamer, J. H. 1965. "Acculturation stress and the functions of alcohol among the Forest Potawatomi." *Quarterly Journal of Studies on Alcohol* 26: 285–302.

————. 1969. "Guardian spirits, alcohol, and cultural defense mechanisms." *Anthropologica*, n.s., 11(2): 215–41.

Haser, S., and White, K. 1969. "The problem of teenage boys on Moen, Truk: A test of a popular diagnosis." In *The Truk Report*, edited by S. Boggs. Honolulu: Department of Anthropology, University of Hawaii.

Hezel, F. X. n.d. "Problem areas in Trukese culture." Unpublished manuscript on file in the Micronesian Seminar Library, Xavier High School, Moen, Truk, Eastern Caroline Islands.

————. 1970. "Catholic missions in the Caroline and Marshall Islands. A survey of historical materials." *Journal of Pacific History* 5: 213–27.

————. 1973*a*. "The beginnings of foreign contact with Truk." *Journal of Pacific History* 8: 51–73.

————. 1973*b*. "The first European visit to Truk." *Guam Recorder*, n.s., 3(3): 38–40.

————. 1976. "Tragic end for troubled youth." *Micronesian Reporter* 24(4): 8–13.

————. 1977. *Micronesia's Youth Today*, edited by F. X. Hezel. A Report on the Conference on Youth Held in Kolonia, Ponape, April 20–24, 1977, Sponsored by the Micronesian Seminar. Moen, Truk: Micronesian Seminar, Xavier High School.

Hocking, R. B. 1970. "Problems arising from alcohol in the New Hebrides." *The Medical Journal of Australia* 2(20): 908–10.

Honigmann, J. L. 1973. "Alcohol in its cultural context." In *Proceedings of the First Annual Alcoholism Conference of the National Institute on Alcohol Abuse and Alcoholism*, edited by M. E. Chafetz, pp. 252–57. Rockville, Maryland: National Institute of Alcohol Abuse and Alcoholism.

Horton, D. 1943. "The functions of alcohol in primitive societies: A cross-cultural study." *Quarterly Journal of Studies on Alcohol* 4: 199–320.

Jack, D. F.; Yangtelmal, C. C.; Reuney, K. S.; and Hadley, S. L. 1977. "Youth of Iras Village." Senior town project, Xavier High School, Moen, Truk. Copy on file in Micronesian Seminar Library, Moen, Truk, Eastern Caroline Islands.

Japan, Nanyō-chō (South Seas Bureau). 1924. *Second Annual Report on Japan's Mandated Territory* (for 1923, to the League of Nations). Geneva: League of Nations.

————. 1927. *Annual Report of the Administration of the South Sea Islands under Japanese Mandate for the Year 1926*. Japan: South Seas Bureau.

————. 1929. *Annual Report to the League of Nations on the Administration of the South Sea Islands under Japanese Mandate for the Year 1928*. Japan: South Seas Bureau.

————. 1931*a*. *Annual Report to the League of Nations on the Administration of the*

South Sea Islands under Japanese Mandate for the Year 1930. Japan: South Seas Bureau.

————. 1931b. *Laws and Regulations Appended to the Annual Report of the Administration of the South Sea Islands under Japanese Mandate for the Year 1930.* Japan: South Seas Bureau.

————. 1931c. *Nanyō Gunto Tōsei Chōsa-sho, Showa 5 nen* [A summary of conditions in the Japanese mandated territories, *1930*]. 4 vols. Palau: Nanyō-chō.

————. 1933. *Annual Report to the League of Nations on the Administration of the South Sea Islands under Japanese Mandate for the year 1932.* Japan: South Seas Bureau.

————. 1934. *Annual Report to the League of Nations on the Administration of the South Sea Islands under Japanese Mandate for the Year 1933.* Japan: South Seas Bureau.

————. 1935. *Annual Report on the Administration of the South Sea Islands under Japanese Mandate for the Year 1934.* Japan: South Seas Bureau.

————. 1936. *Annual Report on the Administration of the South Sea Islands under Japanese Mandate for the Year 1935.* Japan: South Seas Bureau.

————. 1937. *Nanyō Gunto Tōsei Chōsa-sho, Showa 10 nen* [A summary of conditions in the Japanese mandated territories, *1935*]. 2 vols. Tokyo: Nanyō-chō.

Jellinek, E. M. 1960. *The Disease Concept of Alcoholism.* New Haven: College and University Press. New Brunswick, New Jersey: Hillhouse Press.

Kaplan, B., and Johnson, D. 1964. "The social meaning of Navaho psychopathology and psychotherapy." In *Magic, Faith, and Healing,* edited by A. Kiev, pp. 203–29. New York: Free Press.

Kay, A. 1974. "Population growth in Micronesia." *Micronesian Reporter* 22(2): 13–22.

Kay, P. 1963. "Aspects of social structure in a Tahitian urban neighborhood." *Journal of the Polynesian Society* 72: 325–71.

Krämer, A. 1932. "Truk." In *Ergebnisse der Südsee-Expedition, 1908–1910,* edited by G. Thilenius. Vol. 2B5. Hamburg: Friederichsen, de Gruyter & Co.

LeBar, F. M. 1964. *The Material Culture of Truk.* Yale University Publications in Anthropology, No. 68. New Haven: Yale University Press.

Lee, R. B. 1968. "What hunters do for a living, or, how to make out on scarce resources." In *Man the Hunter,* edited by R. B. Lee and I. DeVore, pp. 30–48. Chicago: Aldine.

LeMasters, E. E. 1975. *Blue-Collar Aristocrats: Life-Styles at a Working-Class Tavern.* Madison: University of Wisconsin Press.

Lemert, E. M. 1964. "Forms and pathology of drinking in three Polynesian societies." *American Anthropologist* 66: 361–74.

————. 1976. "Koni, kona, kava. Orange-beer culture of the Cook Islands." *Journal of Studies on Alcohol* 37(5): 565–85.

Leong, P. C. 1953. "The nutritive value of coconut toddy." *The British Journal of Nutrition* 7(3): 253–59.

Levy, J., and Kunitz, S. J. 1974. *Indian Drinking: Navajo Practices and Anglo-*

American Theories. New York: John Wiley & Sons.

Levy, R. 1966. "Ma'ohi drinking patterns in the Society Islands." *Journal of the Polynesian Society* 75: 304–20.

Lewis, D. 1974. "Wind, wave, star, and bird." *National Geographic* 146(6): 747–55, 770–81.

Logan, Rev. R. W. 1886. "Letters from Mr. Logan." *Missionary Herald* 82: 15–18.

———. 1887. "Mission life at Ruk." Ibid. 83: 248–52.

Lutké, F. 1835. *Voyage autour du monde, executé par ordre de sa majeste L'Empereur Nicholas Ier, sur la corvette le seniavine dans les années 1826, 1827, 1828 et 1829.* Vol. 2. Paris: Didot Freres.

MacAndrew, C., and Edgerton, R. B. 1969. *Drunken Comportment: A Social Explanation.* Chicago: Aldine Publishing Co.

MacAndrew, C., and Garfinkel, H. 1962. "A consideration of changes attributed to intoxication as common-sense reasons for getting drunk." *Quarterly Journal of Studies on Alcohol* 23(2): 252–66.

Maccoby, M. 1972. "Alcoholism in a Mexican village." In *The Drinking Man.* edited by D. C. McClelland et al., pp. 232–60. New York: Free Press.

Madsen, W. 1964. *Mexican-Americans of South Texas.* New York: Holt, Rinehart and Winston.

Madsen, W. and Madsen, C. 1969. "The cultural structure of Mexican drinking behavior." *Quarterly Journal of Studies on Alcohol* 30(3): 701–18.

Mahoney, F. B. 1974. *Social and Cultural Factors Relating to the Cause and Control of Alcohol Abuse among Micronesian Youth.* Prepared for the Government of the Trust Territory of the Pacific Islands under Contract TT 174-8 with James R. Leonard Associates, Inc.

Mahony, F. J. 1960. "The innovation of a savings system in Truk." *American Anthropologist* 62(3): 465–82.

Mandelbaum, D. G. 1965. "Alcohol and culture." *Current Anthropology* 6(3): 281–88.

Marianas Variety News & Views 1978. "Surplus liquids to replace liquor in Moen?" *Marianas Variety News & Views,* January 26, 1978 (newspaper published on Saipan, Marianas Islands).

Marshall, M. 1972. "The structure of solidarity and alliance on Namoluk Atoll." Ph.D. dissertation, University of Washington, Seattle.

———. 1975a. "The politics of prohibition on Namoluk Atoll." *Journal of Studies on Alcohol* 36(5):597–610.

———. 1975b. "Changing patterns of marriage and migration on Namoluk Atoll." In *Pacific Atoll Populations,* edited by V. Carroll, pp. 160–211. ASAO Monograph No. 3. Honolulu: University Press of Hawaii.

———. 1976a. "A review and appraisal of alcohol and *kava* studies in Oceania." In *Cross-Cultural Approaches to the Study of Alcohol: An Interdisciplinary Perspective,* edited by M. W. Everett, J. O. Waddell, and D. B. Heath, pp. 103–118. World Anthropology Series. The Hague: Mouton.

———. 1976b. "Solidarity or sterility? Adoption and fosterage on Namoluk Atoll."

In *Transactions in Kinship: Adoption and Fosterage in Oceania*, edited by I. Brady, pp. 28–50. ASAO Monograph No. 4. Honolulu: University Press of Hawaii.

———. 1976c. "The effects of Typhoon Pamela on the Mortlock Islands of Truk District." *Micronesian Reporter* 24(3): 34–39.

———. 1977. "The nature of nurture." *American Ethnologist* 4(4): 643–62.

Marshall, M., and Marshall, L. B. 1975. "Opening Pandora's bottle: Reconstructing Micronesians' early contacts with alcoholic beverages." *Journal of the Polynesian Society* 84(4): 441–65.

———. 1976. "Holy and unholy spirits: The effects of missionization on alcohol use in Eastern Micronesia." *Journal of Pacific History* 11(3): 135–66.

McClelland, D. C.; Davis, W. N.; Kalin, R.; and Wanner, E., eds. 1972. *The Drinking Man: Alcohol and Human Motivation*. New York: The Free Press.

McClelland, D. C.; Davis, W. N.; Wanner, E.; and Kalin, R. 1966. "A cross-cultural study of folk-tale content and drinking." *Sociometry* 29: 308–33.

Micronitor 1971. "Ponapean women demonstrate to keep bars shut." December 14, 1971, p. 1 (a newspaper published in Majuro, Marshall Islands; now called the *Micronesian Independent*).

Missionary Herald 1906. "Our German Co-laborers." *Missionary Herald* 102: 576.

Mohatt, G. 1972. "The sacred water: the quest for personal power through drinking among the Teton Sioux." In *The Drinking Man*, edited by D. C. McClelland et al., pp. 261–75. New York: Free Press.

Murdock, G. P. 1948. "Waging baseball on Truk." *Newsweek* 32(9): 69–70. Reprint 1965. In *Culture and Society: 24 Essays by George P. Murdock*, pp. 291–93. Pittsburgh: University of Pittsburgh Press.

Murdock, G. P., and Goodenough, W. H. 1947. "Social organization of Truk." *Southwestern Journal of Anthropology* 3:331–43.

Nakane, C. 1970. *Japanese Society*. Berkeley and Los Angeles: University of California Press.

Nason, J. D. 1975. "Sardines and other fried fish: The consumption of alcoholic beverages on a Micronesian island." *Journal of Studies on Alcohol* 36(5): 611–25.

Nevin, D. 1977. *The American Touch in Micronesia*. New York: W. W. Norton & Co.

Newman, P. L. 1964. "'Wild-man' behavior in a New Guinea Highlands community." *American Anthropologist* 66(1): 1–19.

Ogan, E. 1966. "Drinking behavior and race relations." *American Anthropologist* 68: 181–88.

Pease, Mrs. 1893. "Journal of Mrs. Pease of Kusaie, Mar. 10–Aug. 22, 1892." *The Friend* 51(2).

Price, W. 1966. *America's Paradise Lost*. New York: John Day.

Prothero, G. W., ed. 1920. *Former German Possessions in Oceania. Handbooks Prepared under the Direction of the Historical Section of the Foreign Office*, No. 146. London: H. M. Stationery Office.

Purcell, D. C. Jr. 1971. "Japanese entrepreneurs in the Mariana, Marshall and Caroline Islands." In *East Across the Pacific: Historical and Sociological Studies of Japanese Immigration and Assimilation,* edited by H. Conroy and T. S. Miyakawa, pp. 56–70. Santa Barbara, California: American Bibliographical Center, Clio Press.

———. 1976. "The economics of exploitation: The Japanese in the Mariana, Caroline and Marshall Islands, 1915–1940." *Journal of Pacific History* 11(3): 189–211.

Raken, I. 1960. "Truk District Congress budget for 1961." *The Truk Review* 2(12): 3–4 (a newspaper formerly published on Moen, Truk, Eastern Caroline Islands).

Richard, D. E. 1957a. *United States Naval Administration of the Trust Territory of the Pacific Islands.* Vol. 1. *The Wartime Military Government Period, 1942–1945.* Washington, D.C.: Office of the Chief of Naval Operations.

———. 1957b. *United States Naval Administration of the Trust Territory of the Pacific Islands.* Vol. 3. *The Trusteeship Period, 1947–1951.* Washington, D.C.: Office of the Chief of Naval Operations.

Robbins, R. H. 1973. "Alcohol and the identity struggle: Some effects of economic change on interpersonal relations." *American Anthropologist* 75(1): 99–122.

Sargent, M. 1967. "Changes in Japanese drinking patterns." *Quarterly Journal of Studies on Alcohol* 28: 709–22.

Schmidt, K. E. 1970. "Excessive alcohol consumption (E.A.C.) in the New Hebrides and recommendations for its management." Noumea: South Pacific Commission. Mimeographed.

Schwartz, T., and Romanucci-Ross, L. 1974. "Drinking and inebriate behavior in the Admiralty Islands, Melanesia." *Ethos* 2(3): 213–31.

Severance, C. J. 1974. "Sanction and sakau: The accessibility and social control of alcohol on Pis-Losap." Paper read at the 3rd Annual Meeting of the Association for Social Anthropology in Oceania, 13–17 March, Asilomar, Pacific Grove, California.

———. 1975. "Becoming Ponapean: The accommodation of the Pis-Losap homesteaders." Paper read at the 4th Annual Meeting of the Association for Social Anthropology in Oceania, 26–30 March, Stuart, Florida.

———. 1976 "Land, food and fish: Strategy and transaction on a Micronesian atoll." Ph.D. dissertation, University of Oregon, Eugene.

Simic, A. 1969. "Management of the male image in Yugoslavia." *Anthropological Quarterly* 42:89–101.

Simmons, O. G. 1960. "Ambivalence and the learning of drinking behavior in a Peruvian community." *American Anthropologist* 62(6): 1018–27.

Spiro, M. E. 1950. "A psychotic personality in the South Seas." *Psychiatry* 13(2): 189–204.

———. 1952. "Ghosts, Ifaluk, and teleological functionalism." *American Anthropologist* 54(4):497–503.

———. 1953. "A typology of functional analysis." *Explorations* 1(1): 84–94.

Swartz, M. J. 1958. "Sexuality and aggression on Romónum, Truk." *American Anthropologist* 60(3): 467–86.

———. 1959. "Leadership and status conflict on Romónum, Truk." *Southwestern Journal of Anthropology* 15(2): 213–18.

———. 1961. "Negative ethnocentrism." *Journal of Conflict Resolution* 5(1):75–81.

———. 1965. "Personality and structure: Political acquiesence in Truk." In *Induced Political Change in the Pacific: A Symposium*, edited by R. W. Force, pp. 17–39. Honolulu: Bishop Museum Press.

Thilenius, G., and Hellwig, F. E. 1927. "Allgemeines; Tagebuch der Expedition; (Die Untersuchung der gesammelten Gesteinsproben by R. Herzenberg)." *Ergebnisse der Südsee-Expedition, 1908–1910*, edited by G. Thilenius. Vol. 1. Hamburg: L. Friederichsen & Co.

Thorner, I. 1953. "Ascetic Protestantism and alcoholism." *Psychiatry* 16(2): 167–76.

Time Magazine 1969. "Anthropology. The original affluent society." *Time*, 25 July, 1969, p. 55.

Tonga, Government of. 1888 *Statistics of the Tonga Islands for the Year ended 31st December, 1887. Trade and Commerce.* Compiled from official records in the Office of the Collector of Customs. Auckland: H. Brett, Printer, The Star Office.

Toomin, P. R., and Toomin, P. M. 1963. *Black Robe and Grass Skirt*. New York: Horizon Press.

Topper, M. D. 1974. "Drinking patterns, culture change, sociability and Navajo 'adolescents'." *Addictive Diseases* 1(1): 97–116.

Treiber, Mr. 1888 "Ruk in 1887–88." *Missionary Herald* 84: 323–26.

Truk Review 1959a "The sale of beers; Local option permitted; Alcoholic Beverage Control Board; Beer tax set at 10¢ for 32 ounces; Hours of sale." *Truk Review* 3(3): 2–3 (May 1959) (a newspaper formerly published on Moen, Truk, Eastern Caroline Islands).

———. 1959b (No title). Ibid 2(5): 5 (November 1959).

United States Department of Health, Education and Welfare (USDHEW) 1973. *HEW/Interior Task Force Report on Health, Sanitation, Education, Social Services in the Trust Territory of the Pacific Islands.* Washington, D.C.: U.S. Department of Health, Education and Welfare.

United States Department of the Navy 1944. *Civil Affairs Handbook, East Caroline Islands.* OPNAV 50E-5. Washington, D.C.: Office of the Chief of Naval Operations.

United States Trust Territory of the Pacific Islands (USTTPI) 1975. *Alcohol and Drug Abuse Plan for the Trust Territory of the Pacific Islands.* Saipan: Division of Mental Health, Department of Health Services.

———. 1976. *1976 Update for the State Alcoholism Plan for the Trust Territory of the Pacific Islands.* Saipan: Division of Mental Health, Department of Health Services.

Wawn, W. T. n.d. Unpublished journal. Original in Alexander Turnbull Library, Wellington, New Zealand. Copy of portion from 1872–1873, during Wawn's sojourn on Ta, Satawan Atoll, available in Micronesian Seminar Library, Xavier High School, Moen, Truk, Eastern Caroline Islands.

Westwood, J. 1905. *Island Stories*. Shanghai: North China Herald Office.

Whiting, R. 1977. *The Chrysanthemum and the Bat. Baseball Samurai Style*. New York: Dodd, Mead.

Whittaker, J. O. 1963. "Alcohol and the Standing Rock Sioux tribe, II: Psychodynamic and cultural factors in drinking." *Quarterly Journal of Studies on Alcohol* 24: 80–90.

Wright, L. B., and Fry, M. I. 1936. *Puritans in the South Seas*. New York: Henry Holt & Co.

Yamamuro, B. 1954. "Notes on drinking in Japan." *Quarterly Journal of Studies on Alcohol* 15: 491–98.

———. 1958 "Japanese drinking patterns: Alcoholic beverages in legend, history and contemporary religions." Ibid. 19: 482–490.

Yanaihara, T. 1940. *Pacific Islands Under Japanese Mandate*. London: Oxford University Press.

Index

Admiralty, Islanders, 52

Aggression, 38, 39–40; and bravery, 56–57; drunkenness as expression of, 46, 47, 52–55, 81, 110–11, 114, 118–23, 126–27; and establishing reputation for competence, 56, 57, 58–60; intergenerational, 110–11; and kung fu movies, 61–63; and *machismo*, 89–94; male masochism in, 96; suicide as, 78–80, 96; in sweetheart relationship, 95–96

Akapito, C., 83, 88

Alcohol: absent from Truk before 1888, 37–38, 40, 103; bar drinking of, 63–64; drinking of, in boonies, 63, 64–64; drinking of, as social act, 64; history of, in Micronesia, 35–50; importation of, 41–42, 43–44, 49, 103; local manufacture of, 40–41, 41–42, 47, 48; prohibition of, 40, 41–50, 152–53; Protestant missionaries on, 32, 33; sale of, 48, 49; school rules about, 21, 70, 143n.5; and sex roles, 65–66, 85–97, 108, 122, 127–28, 130; types of, 51–52,

53 table. *See also* Alcohol abuse; Alcoholism; Drunkenness; *individual beverages by name*

Alcohol abuse: and anxiety, 99–104, 111, 129; case studies of, 67–81; and dependency, 106–9, 111, 129; distinguished from alcoholism, 138n.2; and economic development, 48–49; foreigners as models of comportment for, 35, 44–45, 121; Japanese arrests for, 41, 42–43, 44; and power, 109–11, 129–30; as risk-taking, 59–60; and social class, 30, 123; and social organization, 104–5, 111, 129; treatment for, 133–36; and violent crime, 102–4. *See also* Alcoholism; Drunkenness; Fighting, drunken

Alcoholism, 42, 43, 45, 68, 118, 123, 133, 134, 136, 138n.2

American Board of Commissioners for Foreign Missions (ABCFM), 33, 36–37

American contacts in Micronesia, 32, 33, 34–35, 46–48

Anxiety, and alcohol abuse, 99–104, 111, 129
Automobiles, 6

Bacon, M. K., 106–9, 127
Banana wine, 42
Barry, H. III, 106–9, 127
Bars, 23, 49, 63–64, 66, 83, 84, 88
Baseball, 59
Bateson, G., 131
Beachcombers, 32, 35, 37, 40
Beer (*pio*), 6, 42, 47, 48, 49, 51, 52, 64, 65
Benedict, R., 45
Betel, 35–36
Bingo parlors, 49
Bollig, P., 36, 40
Boonies, drinking in, 63, 64–65, 66, 88
Bourbon, 52, 53 table
Bravery (*pwara*), 56–57, 58, 59–60, 62–63, 71, 77, 80, 96, 97, 120, 130

Canoe trips, ocean, 59
Caroline Islands, 31, 32, 33, 34, 47, 106–7
Catholics, 28
Caughey, Frances, 90
Caughey, J. L. III, 56–58, 93, 95
Cheyne, Andrew, 38
Child, I. L., 106–9, 127
Child rearing, 107–8, 111
Children, 20–21, 81, 94, 108, 116, 122
Chon sakau (village drunks), 30
Chowning, A., 112
Christianity, 36–37. *See also* Catholics; Protestant missionaries
Clans, 24–25, 26, 105. *See also* Kinship; Lineages
Clarke, W. C., 114–15
Clifton, J. A., 105
Coconut toddy (*achi*), 38, 40, 41, 42, 47, 51, 52
Competence, establishing, 56, 57, 58–60, 95, 96, 97, 120, 130
Continental-Travelodge Hotel, 11, 63
Copra plantations, 32, 33
Courage. *See* Bravery
Crime, violent, 102–4

Dailey, R. C., 55
Dennis, P. A., 93, 117
D'Entrecasteaux Islands, 112, 113
Dependency, and alcohol abuse, 106–9, 111, 129
District centers, 6–7, 48–49, 134
Doane, E. T., 37
Dore, R. P., 45
Drinking permits, 60, 63, 64, 93
Drugs, 35–36
Drunkenness: as amok behavior, 112–23; and avoidance, 94; case studies of, 67–81; common themes in, 80–81; composite explanation of, 128–32; as dramatic performance, 30, 80, 113–15, 116–23; as emotional experience, 124–27; and establishing of reputation, 56–57, 58, 60; as excusable behavior, 45, 46, 52–55, 81, 113, 114, 118, 122; foreign models for comportment during, 35, 44–46, 121; incidence of, 68–70; and kung fu movies, 61–63; as learned behavior, 115–18; as *machismo*, 93–94; masochistic elements in, 96; and poolhall, 88; rules for, 122–23; and "sardines," 55, 112, 118–19, 126–27; and social class, 30, 123; as substitute for warfare, 40–41, 46, 52–53, 121, 125, 130; as temporary insanity, 52–55, 80, 88, 113–23; as time out, 45, 46, 113, 122; and Trukese ethos, 131–32; Trukese words for, 51, 53; and Trukese world view, 129, 130–32; as way to express aggression, 46, 47, 52–55, 81, 110–11, 114, 118–23, 126–27; as young man's activity, 65–66, 68, 80, 97, 127–28. *See also* Alcohol abuse; Fighting, drunken; Young men
d'Urville, Dumont, 83

Economic development, 32, 33–34, 48–49, 123
Edgerton, R. B., 113, 115, 117–18, 122
Egalitarianism, 30, 58, 104–5, 123, 129
Ekiyek pwëcëkkün. See Strong thought
Employment, 21, 22 table, 28, 29 table,

Liqueurs, 52, 53 table
Logan, Robert, 37, 39, 57, 141n.9
Love letters, 59
Lütke, Frederic, 82–83, 84

Maasalö clan, 25
MacAndrew, C., 45, 113, 115, 117–18, 120, 122
Maccoby, M., 89, 90, 92
Machismo, 56, 89–94, 109, 120, 125, 126
Madsen, W., 89–90, 123
Mahoney, F. B., 49, 55, 64, 102–3, 114, 117, 134
Maori of New Zealand, 54
Mariana Islands, 34, 103
Marshall Islands, 31, 32–33, 34, 47, 103
Martial arts, 62
Masculinity, 82–85, 89–94, 97, 109, 120, 121, 127–28, 130. *See also* Men; Sex roles; Young men
McClelland, D. C., 109–10
Mecchitiw, 11
Men: drinking of alcohol restricted to, 65–66, 85, 88, 93, 108, 122, 127–28, 130; employment of, 21, 22 table, 29 table; insecurity of, 128, 129; life stages of, and drinking, 64, 65–66, 68, 116; masochism of, 96; poolhall as place of, 23, 86–88; social identity of, 82–85, 89, 97. *See also* Aggression; Drunkenness; Fighting, drunken; Masculinity; Sex roles; Young men
Men's houses, 86–88
Mexico, 89–90, 92, 117
Meyi pwich ("hot stuff"), 51
Moen, 6–11, 26–28, 48, 49–50, 51–53, 60
Mosonoson. See Respectfulness
Mortlock Islands, 24–25, 26, 27 table, 36, 37–38, 54–55, 59
Movie theaters, 14, 17–18, 49
Murdock, G. P., 59, 105
Mwään, 9, 11
Mwääneson (bravery and arrogance), 57

Mwichen asor ("meeting with the supernatural"), 68, 79, 80, 142–43n.3

Nakane, C., 45
Namoluk, 42, 59, 60, 135
Naskapi Indians, 127
Nason, J. D., 58, 118–19
Navajo Indians, 55, 126
Neepwukos, 9
Nevin, D., 61
New Guinea, 54, 112, 113, 114–15, 131
Newman, P. L., 115
Nimitz, Chester W., 46
North American Indian groups, 55

Palau, 47, 48, 103, 105
Palm wine, *See* Coconut toddy
Pease, Mrs., 39
Peniya, 14, 18, 24, 28, 69, 70
Peniyesene, 11, 13, 60, 63, 65; alcohol use and abuse in, 67–81; as bedroom suburb, 18–23; clans in, 24–25, 26; employment in, 21, 22 table, 28, 29 table, 123; government in, 26–28; history of, 24–26; immigration into, 26–27; physical setting of, 14–18; population growth, 26; religion in, 28; schools attended by children from, 20–21; social classes in, 28, 30, 123; social organization of, 26–30
Piis-Losap, 59, 92–93
Police, 26, 70, 76
Ponape, 32, 37, 39, 92–93
Ponape Agricultural and Technical School (PATS), 68
Poolhalls, 14, 17, 23, 48, 69, 70; as men's house, 86–88
Port towns, 6–7. *See also* District centers
Power, and alcohol abuse, 109–11, 129–30
Protestant church (Peniyesene), 14, 18
Protestant missionaries, 32, 33, 36–38, 39
Protestants in Peniyesene, 28
Provincialism, 61
Puluwat Islanders, 40
Pwääng, 61–62

of reputation, 60–61; and Trukese core values, 56–57

Wawn, W. T., 38

Weak thought (*ekiyek pwoteete*), 56, 58, 60, 83–84, 130

Weekend warriors, 57, 63, 67–81, 128–32. See also Aggression; Drunkenness; Fighting, drunken; Young men

Wenikar clan, 24–25

Wesewesen pwara (true bravery), 57

Westwood, John, 36, 38, 119

Whalers, 32, 35, 37, 38

Whiskey, 42, 51, 52, 53 table, 64

Wiichen, 16

Wiitä clan, 25

Wild men of New Guinea, 54, 112, 113, 114–15

Wine (*uain*), 42, 51, 52

Wisiki (distilled spirits), 51

Women: alcohol not drunk by, 65–66, 85, 88, 93, 108, 122, 127–28, 130; and church affairs, 84–85; employment of, 21, 22 table, 29 table; as guardians of the drunk, 81, 93–94; and *machismo*, 91–94; psychological security of, 128, 129; as saintly, 85; in school, 20–21; and tobacco, 85, 130; and weak thought, 58, 60, 83–84. See also Femininity; Sex roles

World War I, 33

World War II, 25–26, 34, 102

Xavier High School, 20, 135

Yamamuro, B., 45

Yap, 103, 105

Yeast. See Homebrew

Young men, 7, 28; aggression in, 110–11, 118–23; and drunkenness, 30, 54, 64–66, 68, 80, 97, 114–15, 116–23, 128–32, 134–36; as irresponsible ne'er-do-wells, 124–27; non-drinkers, 67–68; and schooling, 20–21, 123; and testing of reputation for competence, 56, 57, 58–60, 109, 120, 130; toughness in, 57–58; unemployment of, 28, 123, 134–35. See also Aggression; Drunkenness; Fighting, drunken; Masculinity; Sex roles; Sweetheart relationship

Yugoslavia, 90, 92